MznLnx

Missing Links Exam Preps

Exam Prep for

Calculus: Single and Multivariable

Hughes-Hallett et al., 3rd Edition

The MznLnx Exam Prep is your link from the texbook and lecture to your exams.
The MznLnx Exam Preps are unauthorized and comprehensive reviews of your textbooks.

All material provided by MznLnx and Rico Publications (c) 2010
Textbook publishers and textbook authors do not particpate in or contribute to these reviews.

MznLnx

Rico
Publications

Exam Prep for Calculus: Single and Multivariable
3rd Edition
Hughes-Hallett et al.

Publisher: Raymond Houge
Assistant Editor: Michael Rouger
Text and Cover Designer: Lisa Buckner
Marketing Manager: Sara Swagger
Project Manager, Editorial Production: Jerry Emerson
Art Director: Vernon Lowerui

Product Manager: Dave Mason
Editorial Assitant: Rachel Guzmanji
Pedagogy: Debra Long
Cover Image: Jim Reed/Getty Images
Text and Cover Printer: City Printing, Inc.
Compositor: Media Mix, Inc.

(c) 2010 Rico Publications
ALL RIGHTS RESERVED. No part of this work
covered by the copyright may be reproduced or
used in any form or by an means--graphic, electronic,
or mechanical, including photocopying, recording,
taping, Web distribution, information storage, and
retrieval systems, or in any other manner--without the
written permission of the publisher.

Printed in the United States
ISBN:

For more information about our products, contact us at:
Dave.Mason@RicoPublications.com

For permission to use material from this text or
product, submit a request online to:
Dave.Mason@RicoPublications.com

Contents

CHAPTER 1
A LIBRARY OF FUNCTIONS — 1

CHAPTER 2
KEY CONCEPT: THE DERIVATIVE — 16

CHAPTER 3
SHORT-CUTS TO DIFFERENTIATION — 22

CHAPTER 4
USING THE DERIVATIVE — 30

CHAPTER 5
KEY CONCEPT: THE DEFINITE INTEGRAL — 38

CHAPTER 6
CONSTRUCTING ANTIDERIVATIVES — 42

CHAPTER 7
INTEGRATION — 46

CHAPTER 8
USING THE DEFINITE INTEGRAL — 57

CHAPTER 9
SERIES — 63

CHAPTER 10
APPROXIMATING FUNCTIONS — 68

CHAPTER 11
DIFFERENTIAL EQUATIONS — 75

CHAPTER 12
FUNCTIONS OF SEVERAL VARIABLES — 85

CHAPTER 13
A FUNDAMENTAL TOOL: VECTORS — 90

CHAPTER 14
DIFFERENTIATING FUNCTIONS OF SEVERAL VARIABLES — 95

CHAPTER 15
OPTIMIZATION: LOCAL AND GLOBAL EXTREMA — 102

CHAPTER 16
INTEGRATING FUNCTIONS OF SEVERAL VARIABLES — 108

CHAPTER 17
PARAMETERIZATION AND VECTOR FIELDS — 113

CHAPTER 18
LINE INTEGRALS — 117

CHAPTER 19
FLUX INTEGRALS — 121

CHAPTER 20
CALCULUS OF VECTOR FIELDS — 124

ANSWER KEY — 134

TO THE STUDENT

COMPREHENSIVE

The *MznLnx* Exam Prep series is designed to help you pass your exams. Editors at MznLnx review your textbooks and then prepare these practice exams to help you master the textbook material. Unlike study guides, workbooks, and practice tests provided by the texbook publisher and textbook authors, *MznLnx* gives you **all** of the material in each chapter in exam form, not just samples, so you can be sure to nail your exam.

MECHANICAL

The MznLnx Exam Prep series creates exams that will help you learn the subject matter as well as test you on your understanding. Each question is designed to help you master the concept. Just working through the exams, you gain an understanding of the subject--its a simple mechanical process that produces success.

INTEGRATED STUDY GUIDE AND REVIEW

MznLnx is not just a set of exams designed to test you, its also a comprehensive review of the subject content. Each exam question is also a review of the concept, making sure that you will get the answer correct without having to go to other sources of material. You learn as you go! Its the easiest way to pass an exam.

HUMOR

Studying can be tedious and dry. MznLnx's instructional design includes moderate humor within the exam questions on occassion, to break the tedium and revitalize the brain

Chapter 1. A LIBRARY OF FUNCTIONS 1

1. The terms '_____' and 'independent variable' are used in similar but subtly different ways in mathematics and statistics as part of the standard terminology in those subjects. They are used to distinguish between two types of quantities being considered, separating them into those available at the start of a process and those being created by it, where the latter (dependent variables) are dependent on the former (independent variables.)

In traditional calculus, a function is defined as a relation between two terms called variables because their values vary.

a. 15 theorem
b. BIBO stability
c. BDDC
d. Dependent variable

2. _____ arise in the mathematical description of probabilistic and statistical problems in which the values that might be observed are restricted to being within a pre-defined list of possible values. This list has either a finite number of members, or at most is countable.

In probability theory, a probability distribution is called discrete if it is characterized by a probability mass function.

a. Correlation
b. Continuous random variable
c. Linear regression
d. Discrete probability distributions

3. In mathematics, the _____ (or replacement set) of a given function is the set of 'input' values for which the function is defined. For instance, the _____ of cosine would be all real numbers, while the _____ of the square root would be only numbers greater than or equal to 0 (ignoring complex numbers in both cases.) In a representation of a function in a xy Cartesian coordinate system, the _____ is represented on the x axis (or abscissa.)

a. BIBO stability
b. BDDC
c. 15 theorem
d. Domain

4. In mathematics, a _____ decomposes a periodic function into a sum of simple oscillating functions, namely sines and cosines (or complex exponentials.) The study of _____ is a branch of Fourier analysis. _____ were introduced by Joseph Fourier (1768-1830) for the purpose of solving the heat equation in a metal plate.

a. 15 theorem
b. BDDC
c. BIBO stability
d. Fourier series

5. The terms 'dependent variable' and '_____' are used in similar but subtly different ways in mathematics and statistics as part of the standard terminology in those subjects. They are used to distinguish between two types of quantities being considered, separating them into those available at the start of a process and those being created by it, where the latter (dependent variables) are dependent on the former (independent variables.)

In traditional calculus, a function is defined as a relation between two terms called variables because their values vary.

a. ACTRAN
b. ALGOR
c. AUSM
d. Independent variable

6. The _____, L, of a dynamical system is a function that summarizes the dynamics of the system. It is named after Joseph Louis Lagrange. The concept of a _____ was originally introduced in a reformulation of classical mechanics known as _____ mechanics.
   a. Klein-Gordon equation
   b. Vector potential
   c. Lagrangian
   d. Dirac equation

7. In mathematics, the _____ of a function is the set of all 'output' values produced by that function. Sometimes it is called the image, or more precisely, the image of the domain of the function. If a function is a surjection then its _____ is equal to its codomain.
   a. Surjective
   b. Piecewise-defined function
   c. Constant function
   d. Range

8. In mathematics, _____ is the process of constructing new data points outside a discrete set of known data points. It is similar to the process of interpolation, which constructs new points between known points, but the results of extrapolations are often less meaningful, and are subject to greater uncertainty. Example illustration of the _____ problem, consisting of assigning a meaningful value at the blue box, at x = 7, given the red data points.

   A sound choice of which _____ method to apply relies on a prior knowledge of the process that created the existing data points.

   a. ALGOR
   b. AUSM
   c. ACTRAN
   d. Extrapolation

9. In economics, the _____ functional form of production functions is widely used to represent the relationship of an output to inputs. It was proposed by Knut Wicksell (1851-1926), and tested against statistical evidence by Charles Cobb and Paul Douglas in 1900-1928.

For production, the function is

$$Y = AL^{\alpha}K^{\beta},$$

where:

- Y = total production (the monetary value of all goods produced in a year)
- L = labor input
- K = capital input
- A = total factor productivity
- α and β are the output elasticities of labor and capital, respectively. These values are constants determined by available technology.

Output elasticity measures the responsiveness of output to a change in levels of either labor or capital used in production, ceteris paribus. For example if α = 0.15, a 1% increase in labor would lead to approximately a 0.15% increase in output.

Chapter 1. A LIBRARY OF FUNCTIONS

a. BIBO stability
c. 15 theorem
b. BDDC
d. Cobb-Douglas

10. The function difference divided by the point difference is known as the _____, it is also known as Newton's quotient):

$$\frac{\Delta F(P)}{\Delta P} = \frac{F(P + \Delta P) - F(P)}{\Delta P} = \frac{\nabla F(P + \Delta P)}{\Delta P}.$$

If ΔP is infinitesimal, then the _____ is a derivative, otherwise it is a divided difference:

$$\text{If } |\Delta P| = iota: \quad \frac{\Delta F(P)}{\Delta P} = \frac{dF(P)}{dP} = F'(P) = G(P);$$

$$\text{If } |\Delta P| > iota: \quad \frac{\Delta F(P)}{\Delta P} = \frac{DF(P)}{DP} = F[P, P + \Delta P].$$

Regardless if ΔP is infinitesimal or finite, there is (at least--in the case of the derivative--theoretically) a point range, where the boundaries are P ± (.5)ΔP (depending on the orientation--ΔF(P), δF(P) or ∇F(P)):

    LB = Lower Boundary; UB = Upper Boundary;

Anyone familiar with derivatives knows that they can be regarded as functions themselves, harboring their own derivatives. Thus each function is home to sequential degrees ('higher orders') of derivation, or differentiation. This property can be generalized to all difference quotients.As this sequencing requires a corresponding boundary splintering, it is practical to break up the point range into smaller, equi-sized sections, with each section being marked by an intermediary point ('P_i'), where LB = P_0 and UB = P_{A_n}, the nth point, equaling the degree/order:

LB = P_0 = P_0 + 0Δ_1P = P_{A_n} - (Åƒ-0)Δ_1P; P_1 = P_0 + 1Δ_1P = P_{A_n} - (Åƒ-1)Δ_1P; P_2 = P_0 + 2Δ_1P = P_{A_n} - (Åƒ-2)Δ_1P; P_3 = P_0 + 3Δ_1P = P_{A_n} - (Åƒ-3)Δ_1P; ↓↓↓↓ P_{A_n-3} = P_0 + (Åƒ-3)Δ_1P = P_{A_n} - 3Δ_1P; P_{A_n-2} = P_0 + (Åƒ-2)Δ_1P = P_{A_n} - 2Δ_1P; P_{A_n-1} = P_0 + (Åƒ-1)Δ_1P = P_{A_n} - 1Δ_1P; UB = P_{A_n-0} = P_0 + (Åƒ-0)Δ_1P = P_{A_n} - 0Δ_1P = P_{A_n};

ΔP = Δ_1P = P_1 - P_0 = P_2 - P_1 = P_3 - P_2 = ...

a. Continuously differentiable
c. Directional derivative
b. Notation for differentiation
d. Difference quotient

Chapter 1. A LIBRARY OF FUNCTIONS

11. In mathematics, a (topological) _____ is defined as follows: let I be an interval of real numbers (i.e. a non-empty connected subset of $\mathbb{R}$); then a _____ γ is a continuous mapping $\gamma : I \to X$, where X is a topological space. The _____ γ is said to be simple if it is injective, i.e. if for all x, y in I, we have $\gamma(x) = \gamma(y) \implies x = y$. If I is a closed bounded interval $[a, b]$, we also allow the possibility $\gamma(a) = \gamma(b)$ (this convention makes it possible to talk about closed simple _____.)

  a. Tractrix
  b. Prolate cycloid
  c. Closed curve
  d. Curve

12. is called the proportionality constant or _____.

- If an object travels at a constant speed, then the distance traveled is proportional to the time spent travelling, with the speed being the _____.

- The circumference of a circle is proportional to its diameter, with the _____ equal to π.

- On a map drawn to scale, the distance between any two points on the map is proportional to the distance between the two locations that the points represent, with the _____ being the scale of the map.

- The force acting on a certain object due to gravity is proportional to the object's mass; the _____ between the the mass and the force is known as gravitational acceleration.

Since

$$y = kx$$

is equivalent to

$$x = \left(\frac{1}{k}\right) y,$$

it follows that if y is proportional to x, with (nonzero) proportionality constant k, then x is also proportional to y with proportionality constant 1/k.

If y is proportional to x, then the graph of y as a function of x will be a straight line passing through the origin with the slope of the line equal to the _____: it corresponds to linear growth.

  a. Reduction
  b. 15 theorem
  c. BDDC
  d. Constant of proportionality

13. In mathematics, a _____ is a function which preserves the given order. This concept first arose in calculus, and was later generalized to the more abstract setting of order theory.

Chapter 1. A LIBRARY OF FUNCTIONS 5

In calculus, a function f defined on a subset of the real numbers with real values is called monotonic (also monotonically increasing or non-decreasing), if for all x and y such that x >≤ y one has f(x) >≤ f(y), so f preserves the order.

a. 15 theorem
b. Pettis integral
c. Pseudo-differential operator
d. Monotonic function

14. Two variables are _____ if one of the variables is directly proportional with the multiplicative inverse (reciprocal) of the other the concept of inverse proportion means that as the absolute value or magnitude of one variable gets bigger, the absolute value or magnitude of another gets smaller, such that their product (the constant of proportionality) is always the same.
a. AUSM
b. ALGOR
c. ACTRAN
d. Inversely proportional

15. The _____ is a function in mathematics. The application of this function to a value x is written as exp(x). Equivalently, this can be written in the form e^x, where e is a mathematical constant, the base of the natural logarithm, which equals approximately 2.718281828, and is also known as Euler's number.
a. Integral part
b. Exponential function
c. Area hyperbolic functions
d. ACTRAN

16. _____ (including exponential decay) occurs when the growth rate of a mathematical function is proportional to the function's current value. In the case of a discrete domain of definition with equal intervals it is also called geometric growth or geometric decay (the function values form a geometric progression.)

_____ is said to follow an exponential law; the simple-_____ model is known as the Malthusian growth model.

a. Exponential growth
b. Inseparable differential equation
c. Oscillating
d. Isomonodromic deformation

17. A quantity is said to be subject to _____ if it decreases at a rate proportional to its value. Symbolically, this can be expressed as the following differential equation, where N is the quantity and λ is a positive number called the decay constant.

$$\frac{dN}{dt} = -\lambda N.$$

The solution to this equation is:

$$N(t) = N_0 e^{-\lambda t}.$$

Here N(t) is the quantity at time t, and $N_0 = N(0)$ is the initial quantity, i.e. the quantity at time t = 0.

a. Exponential sum
b. ALGOR
c. ACTRAN
d. Exponential decay

18. The _____ of a quantity whose value decreases with time is the interval required for the quantity to decay to half of its initial value. The concept originated in describing how long it takes atoms to undergo radioactive decay but also applies in a wide variety of other situations.

The term '_____' dates to 1907.

a. 15 theorem
b. BDDC
c. BIBO stability
d. Half-life

19. In mathematics, a _____ represents the application of one function to the results of another. For instance, the functions f: X → Y and g: Y → Z can be composed by first computing f(x) and then applying a function g to the output of f(x).

Thus one obtains a function g ∘ f: X → Z defined by (g ∘ f)(x) = g(f(x)) for all x in X. The notation g ∘ f is read as 'g circle f', or 'g composed with f', 'g after f', 'g following f', or just 'g of f'.

a. Piecewise-defined function
b. Constant function
c. Surjective
d. Composite function

20. In mathematics, even functions and odd functions are functions which satisfy particular symmetry relations, with respect to taking additive inverses. They are important in many areas of mathematical analysis, especially the theory of power series and Fourier series. They are named for the parity of the powers of the power functions which satisfy each condition: the function $f(x) = x^n$ is an _____ if n is an even integer, and it is an odd function if n is an odd integer.

a. Integral of secant cubed
b. Infinite series
c. Even function
d. Operational calculus

21. In mathematics, the _____ of a function y = f(x) is a function that, in some fashion, 'undoes' the effect of f The _____ of f is denoted f^{-1}. The statements y=f(x) and x=f^{-1}(y) are equivalent.

a. Inverse
b. AUSM
c. ALGOR
d. ACTRAN

22. In mathematics, if f is a function from A to B then an _____ for f is a function in the opposite direction, from B to A, with the property that a round trip (a composition) from A to B to A (or from B to A to B) returns each element of the initial set to itself. Thus, if an input x into the function f produces an output y, then inputting y into the _____ f^{-1} (read f inverse, not to be confused with exponentiation) produces the output x. Not every function has an inverse; those that do are called invertible.

a. Inverse function
b. Augustin Louis Cauchy
c. Augustin-Jean Fresnel
d. Aristotle

23. In mathematics, even functions and odd functions are functions which satisfy particular symmetry relations, with respect to taking additive inverses. They are important in many areas of mathematical analysis, especially the theory of power series and Fourier series. They are named for the parity of the powers of the power functions which satisfy each condition: the function $f(x) = x^n$ is an even function if n is an even integer, and it is an _____ if n is an odd integer.

a. Integration by substitution
c. Odd function
b. Even function
d. Integral of secant cubed

24. _____ generally conveys two primary meanings. The first is an imprecise sense of harmonious or aesthetically-pleasing proportionality and balance; such that it reflects beauty or perfection. The second meaning is a precise and well-defined concept of balance or 'patterned self-similarity' that can be demonstrated or proved according to the rules of a formal system: by geometry, through physics or otherwise.
   a. BIBO stability
   c. BDDC
   b. Symmetry
   d. 15 theorem

25. In mathematics, the _____ is a test used to determine if a function is injective, surjective or bijective.

Suppose there is a function f : X → Y with a graph., and you have a horizontal line of X x Y :
$$y_0 \in Y, \{(x, y_0) : x \in X\} = (X \times y_0)$$.

- If the function is injective, then it can be visualized as one whose graph is never intersected by any horizontal line more than once.
- If and only if f is surjective, any horizontal line will intersect the graph at least at one point (when the horizontal line is in the codomain.)
- If f is bijective, any horizontal line will intersect the graph at exactly one point.

This test is also used to find whether or not the inverse of the function is indeed a function as well. This is due to the reflective properties of the function over y=x.

   a. 15 theorem
   c. BIBO stability
   b. Horizontal line test
   d. BDDC

26. Let S be a set with a binary operation * . If e is an identity element of (S, *) and a * b = e, then a is called a _____ of b and b is called a right inverse of a. If an element x is both a _____ and a right inverse of y, then x is called a two-sided inverse, or simply an inverse, of y.
   a. Left inverse
   c. Closed-form expression
   b. Completing the square
   d. Hurwitz quaternion order

27. The natural logarithm, formerly known as the hyperbolic logarithm, is the logarithm to the _____, where e is an irrational constant approximately equal to 2.718281828. It is also sometimes referred to as the Napierian logarithm, although the original meaning of this term is slightly different. In simple terms, the natural logarithm of a number x is the power to which e would have to be raised to equal x -- for example the natural log of e itself is 1 because e^1 = e, while the natural logarithm of 1 would be 0, since e^0 = 1.
   a. 15 theorem
   c. BIBO stability
   b. Base e
   d. BDDC

28. The function $\log_b(x)$ depends on both b and x, but the term _____ in standard usage refers to a function of the form $\log_b(x)$ in which the base b is fixed and so the only argument is x. Thus there is one _____ for each value of the base b (which must be positive and must differ from 1.) Viewed in this way, the base-b _____ is the inverse function of the exponential function b^x.

Chapter 1. A LIBRARY OF FUNCTIONS

a. 15 theorem
c. BDDC

b. Logarithm function
d. BIBO stability

29. In mathematics, the _____ is a representation of a function as an infinite sum of terms calculated from the values of its derivatives at a single point. It may be regarded as the limit of the Taylor polynomials. If the series is centered at zero, the series is also called a Maclaurin series.

a. BIBO stability
c. BDDC

b. 15 theorem
d. Taylor series

30. An _____ of a real-valued function y = f(x) is a curve which describes the behavior of f as either x or y tends to infinity.

In other words, as one moves along the graph of f(x) in some direction, the distance between it and the _____ eventually becomes smaller than any distance that one may specify.

a. ALGOR
c. ACTRAN

b. Asymptote
d. AUSM

31. In calculus, a branch of mathematics, the _____ is a measurement of how a function changes when its input changes. Loosely speaking, a _____ can be thought of as how much a quantity is changing at some given point. For example, the _____ of the position (or distance) of a vehicle with respect to time is the instantaneous velocity (respectively, instantaneous speed) at which the vehicle is traveling.

The process of finding a _____ is called differentiation. The fundamental theorem of calculus states that differentiation is the reverse process to integration.

a. Bounded function
c. Semi-differentiability

b. Derivative
d. Stationary phase approximation

32. The line x = a is a _____ of a curve y=f(x) if at least one of the following statements is true:

1. $\lim_{x \to a} f(x) = \pm\infty$
2. $\lim_{x \to a^-} f(x) = \pm\infty$
3. $\lim_{x \to a^+} f(x) = \pm\infty$

Intuitively, if x = a is an asymptote of f, then, if we imagine x approaching a from one side, the value of f(x) grows without bound; i.e., f(x) becomes large (positively or negatively), and, in fact, becomes larger than any finite value.

Note that f(x) may or may not be defined at a: what the function is doing precisely at x = a does not affect the asymptote. For example, consider the function

$$f(x) = \begin{cases} \frac{1}{x} & \text{if } x > 0, \\ 5 & \text{if } x \leq 0 \end{cases}$$

As $\lim_{x \to 0^+} f(x) = \infty$, f(x) has a _____ at 0, even though f(0) = 5.

Another example is $f(x) = 1/(x-1)$ which has a _____ of x=1 as shown by the limit

$$\lim_{x \to 1^+} \frac{1}{x-1} = \infty$$

In the graph of $f(x) = x + \frac{1}{x}$, the y-axis (x = 0) and the line y = x are both asymptotes.

When a linear asymptote is not parallel to the x- or y-axis, it is called either an oblique asymptote or equivalently a slant asymptote.

a. Third derivative
c. Ramp function
b. Monodromy
d. Vertical asymptote

33. Trigonometry is a branch of mathematics that deals with triangles, particularly those plane triangles in which one angle has 90 degrees (right triangles.) Trigonometry deals with relationships between the sides and the angles of triangles and with the _____ functions, which describe those relationships.

Trigonometry has applications in both pure mathematics and in applied mathematics, where it is essential in many branches of science and technology.

a. Trigonometric functions
c. Trigonometric integrals
b. Trigonometric
d. Sine

34. In mathematics, the _____ are functions of an angle. They are important in the study of triangles and modeling periodic phenomena, among many other applications. _____ are commonly defined as ratios of two sides of a right triangle containing the angle, and can equivalently be defined as the lengths of various line segments from a unit circle.

a. Trigonometric
c. Sine integral
b. Trigonometric integrals
d. Trigonometric functions

35. The _____ of an angle is the ratio of the length of the opposite side to the length of the hypotenuse. In our case

Chapter 1. A LIBRARY OF FUNCTIONS

$$\sin A = \frac{\text{opposite}}{\text{hypotenuse}} = \frac{a}{h}.$$

Note that this ratio does not depend on size of the particular right triangle chosen, as long as it contains the angle A, since all such triangles are similar.

The cosine of an angle is the ratio of the length of the adjacent side to the length of the hypotenuse.

a. Trigonometric
b. Sine integral
c. Trigonometric functions
d. Sine

36. In mathematics, trigonometric identities are equalities that involve trigonometric functions that are true for every single value of the occurring variables. These identities are useful whenever expressions involving trigonometric functions need to be simplified. An important application is the integration of non-trigonometric functions: a common technique involves first using the substitution rule with a trigonometric function, and then simplifying the resulting integral with a _____.

a. 15 theorem
b. BDDC
c. BIBO stability
d. Trigonometric identity

37. In mathematics, a _____ is a circle with a unit radius, i.e., a circle whose radius is 1. Frequently, especially in trigonometry, 'the' _____ is the circle of radius 1 centered at the origin (0, 0) in the Cartesian coordinate system in the Euclidean plane. The _____ is often denoted S^1; the generalization to higher dimensions is the unit sphere.

a. ACTRAN
b. ALGOR
c. AUSM
d. Unit circle

38. In mathematics, the _____ or cyclometric functions are the inverse functions of the trigonometric functions. The principal inverses are listed in the following table.

If x is allowed to be a complex number, then the range of y applies only to its real part.

a. ALGOR
b. AUSM
c. ACTRAN
d. Inverse trigonometric functions

39. In geometry, the _____ (or simply the tangent) to a curve at a given point is the straight line that 'just touches' the curve at that point (in the sense explained more precisely below.) As it passes through the point of tangency, the _____ is 'going in the same direction' as the curve, and in this sense it is the best straight-line approximation to the curve at that point. The same definition applies to space curves and curves in n-dimensional Euclidean space.

a. North pole
b. Lie derivative
c. Minimal surface
d. Tangent line

40. When a polynomial is expressed as a sum or difference of terms (e.g., in standard or canonical form), the exponent of the term with the highest exponent is the _____. The degree of a term is the sum of the powers of each variable in the term. The words degree and order are used interchangeably.

Chapter 1. A LIBRARY OF FUNCTIONS

a. Symmetric function	b. Quadratic polynomial
c. Binomial type	d. Degree of the polynomial

41. In mathematics, a _____ or quadratic is a polynomial of degree two. A _____ may involve a single variable x, or multiple variables such as x, y, and z.

Any single-variable _____ may be written as

$$ax^2 + bx + c,$$

where x is the variable, and a, b, and c represent the coefficients.

a. Binomial type	b. Difference polynomial
c. Characteristic equation	d. Quadratic polynomial

42. In mathematics and elsewhere, the adjective _____ means 'fourth order', such as the function x^4. A _____ number is a number which equals the fourth power of an integer.

a. 15 theorem	b. Quartic
c. BDDC	d. Reduction

43. In mathematics, a _____ is a function of the form

$$f(x) = ax^4 + bx^3 + cx^2 + dx + e$$

where a is nonzero; or in other words, a polynomial of degree of four. Such a function is sometimes called a biquadratic function, but the latter term can occasionally also refer to a quadratic function of a square, having the form

$$ax^4 + bx^2 + c,$$

or a product of two quadratic factors, having the form

$$(ax^2 + bx + c)(dy^2 + ey + f).$$

If you set f(x) = 0, you get a quartic equation of the form:

$$ax^4 + bx^3 + cx^2 + dx + e = 0$$

where a ≠ 0.

The derivative of a _____ is a cubic function.

a. Linear equation
c. Quadratic formula
b. Cubic function
d. Quartic function

44. In mathematics, a _____ equation is a polynomial equation of degree five. It is of the form:

$$ax^5 + bx^4 + cx^3 + dx^2 + ex + f = 0,$$

where $a \neq 0$.

(if a = 0, then the equation becomes a quartic equation.)(if a and b = 0, then the equation becomes a cubic equation.)(if a, b and c = 0, then the equation becomes a quadratic equation.)(if a, b, c and d = 0, then the equation becomes a linear equation.)

a. Quintic
c. BIBO stability
b. 15 theorem
d. BDDC

45. In mathematics, a _____ is a polynomial equation of degree five. It is of the form:

$$ax^5 + bx^4 + cx^3 + dx^2 + ex + f = 0,$$

where $a \neq 0$.

(if a = 0, then the equation becomes a quartic equation.)(if a and b = 0, then the equation becomes a cubic equation.)(if a, b and c = 0, then the equation becomes a quadratic equation.)(if a, b, c and d = 0, then the equation becomes a linear equation.)

a. BDDC
c. 15 theorem
b. Quintic equation
d. BIBO stability

46. In mathematics, the _____ is a conic section, the intersection of a right circular conical surface and a plane parallel to a generating straight line of that surface. Given a point (the focus) and a line (the directrix) that lie in a plane, the locus of points in that plane that are equidistant to them is a _____.

A particular case arises when the plane is tangent to the conical surface of a circle.

a. 15 theorem
c. BDDC
b. BIBO stability
d. Parabola

47. Suppose f is a function. Then the line y = a is a _____ for f if

$$\lim_{x \to \infty} f(x) = a \text{ or } \lim_{x \to -\infty} f(x) = a.$$

Intuitively, this means that f(x) can be made as close as desired to a by making x big enough. How big is big enough depends on how close one wishes to make f(x) to a.

- a. Second derivative
- b. Mountain pass theorem
- c. Horizontal asymptote
- d. Third derivative

48. In mathematics, a _____ is any function which can be written as the ratio of two polynomial functions.

$$y = \frac{x^2 - 3x - 2}{x^2 - 4}$$

In the case of one variable, x, a _____ is a function of the form

$$f(x) = \frac{P(x)}{Q(x)}$$

where P and Q are polynomial function in x and Q is not the zero polynomial. The domain of f is the set of all points x for which the denominator Q(x) is not zero.

- a. BIBO stability
- b. BDDC
- c. Rational function
- d. 15 theorem

49. In mathematics, a _____ is a constant multiplicative factor of a certain object. For example, in the expression $9x^2$, the _____ of x^2 is 9.

The object can be such things as a variable, a vector, a function, etc.

- a. Binomial type
- b. Resultant
- c. Degree of the polynomial
- d. Coefficient

50. For the largest k where $a_k \neq 0$, a_k is called the _____ of P because most often, polynomials are written starting from the left with the largest power of x. So for example the _____ of the polynomial

$$4x^5 + x^3 + 2x^2$$

is 4.

The coefficients of polynomial also may be in the other order:

$$Q(x) = a_0 x^k + a_1 x^{k-1} + \cdots + a_{k-1} x^1 + a_k$$

and must be $a_0 \neq 0$ and a_0 is the _____ of Q.

a. Discriminant
b. Symmetric function
c. Resultant
d. Leading coefficient

51. In mathematical analysis, the _____ states that for each value between the least upper bound and greatest lower bound of the image of a continuous function there is a corresponding value in its domain mapping to the original. _____

- Version I. The _____ states the following: If the function y = f(x) is continuous on the interval [a, b], and u is a number between f(a) and f(b), then there is a c ∈ [a, b] such that f(c) = u.

- Version II. Suppose that I is an interval [a, b] in the real numbers R and that f : I → R is a continuous function. Then the image set f(I) is also an interval, and either it contains [f(a), f(b)], or it contains [f(b), f(a)]; that is,

    f(I) ⊇ [f(a), f(b)], or f(I) ⊇ [f(b), f(a)].

It is frequently stated in the following equivalent form: Suppose that f : [a, b] → R is continuous and that u is a real number satisfying f(a) < u < f(b) or f(a) > u > f(b).) Then for some c ∈ [a, b], f(c) = u.

This captures an intuitive property of continuous functions: given f continuous on [1, 2], if f(1) = 3 and f(2) = 5 then f must take the value 4 somewhere between 1 and 2.

a. ALGOR
b. Intermediate Value Theorem
c. AUSM
d. ACTRAN

52. _____ was a German mathematician, astronomer and astrologer, and key figure in the 17th century scientific revolution. He is best known for his eponymous laws of planetary motion, codified by later astronomers based on his works Astronomia nova, Harmonices Mundi, and Epitome of Copernican Astrononomy. They also provided one of the foundations for Isaac Newton's theory of universal gravitation.

a. Niels Henrik David Bohr
b. MÄ dhava of Sangamagrama
c. Robin K. Bullough
d. Johannes Kepler

53. In geometry, the _____ (also semimajor axis) is used to describe the dimensions of ellipses and hyperbolae.

The major axis of an ellipse is its longest diameter, a line that runs through the centre and both foci, its ends being at the widest points of the shape. The _____ is one half of the major axis, and thus runs from the centre, through a focus, and to the edge of the ellipse.

a. 15 theorem
b. BDDC
c. BIBO stability
d. Semi-major axis

54. _____ is the concept of adding accumulated interest back to the principal, so that interest is earned on interest from that moment on. The act of declaring interest to be principal is called compounding (i.e., interest is compounded.) A loan, for example, may have its interest compounded every month: in this case, a loan with $100 principal and 1% interest per month would have a balance of $101 at the end of the first month.

   a. BDDC   b. Compound interest

   c. 15 theorem   d. BIBO stability

Chapter 2. KEY CONCEPT: THE DERIVATIVE

1. In physics, _____ is defined as the rate of change of position. it is vector physical quantity; both speed and direction are required to define it. In the SI (metric) system, it is measured in meters per second: (m/s) or ms^{-1}.
   a. BIBO stability
   b. 15 theorem
   c. Velocity
   d. BDDC

2. In mathematics, a (topological) _____ is defined as follows: let I be an interval of real numbers (i.e. a non-empty connected subset of $\mathbb{R}$); then a _____ γ is a continuous mapping $\gamma : I \to X$, where X is a topological space. The _____ γ is said to be simple if it is injective, i.e. if for all x, y in I, we have $\gamma(x) = \gamma(y) \implies x = y$. If I is a closed bounded interval $[a, b]$, we also allow the possibility $\gamma(a) = \gamma(b)$ (this convention makes it possible to talk about closed simple _____.)
   a. Closed curve
   b. Prolate cycloid
   c. Tractrix
   d. Curve

3. In mathematics, the concept of a '_____' is used to describe the behavior of a function as its argument or input either 'gets close' to some point, or as the argument becomes arbitrarily large; or the behavior of a sequence's elements as their index increases indefinitely. Limits are used in calculus and other branches of mathematical analysis to define derivatives and continuity.

   In formulas, _____ is usually abbreviated as lim

   a. BIBO stability
   b. Limit
   c. 15 theorem
   d. BDDC

4. In calculus, a _____ is either of the two limits of a function f(x) of a real variable x as x approaches a specified point either from below or from above. One should write either:

$$\lim_{x \to a^+} f(x) \text{ or } \lim_{x \downarrow a} f(x)$$

for the limit as x decreases in value approaching a (x approaches a 'from above' or 'from the right'), and similarly

$$\lim_{x \to a^-} f(x) \text{ or } \lim_{x \uparrow a} f(x)$$

for the limit as x increases in value approaching a (x approaches a 'from below' or 'from the left'.)

The two one-sided limits exist and are equal if and only if the limit of f(x) as x approaches a exists.

   a. AUSM
   b. ALGOR
   c. ACTRAN
   d. One-sided limit

5. In mathematics, a _____ is a function whose values do not vary and thus are constant. For example, if we have the function f(x) = 4, then f is constant since f maps any value to 4. More formally, a function f : A → B is a _____ if f(x) = f(y) for all x and y in A.

Chapter 2. KEY CONCEPT: THE DERIVATIVE

a. Surjective
b. Constant function
c. Range
d. Piecewise-defined function

6. An _____ of a real-valued function y = f(x) is a curve which describes the behavior of f as either x or y tends to infinity. In other words, as one moves along the graph of f(x) in some direction, the distance between it and the _____ eventually becomes smaller than any distance that one may specify.

a. ALGOR
b. ACTRAN
c. AUSM
d. Asymptote

7. In calculus, a branch of mathematics, the _____ is a measurement of how a function changes when its input changes. Loosely speaking, a _____ can be thought of as how much a quantity is changing at some given point. For example, the _____ of the position (or distance) of a vehicle with respect to time is the instantaneous velocity (respectively, instantaneous speed) at which the vehicle is traveling.

The process of finding a _____ is called differentiation. The fundamental theorem of calculus states that differentiation is the reverse process to integration.

a. Semi-differentiability
b. Stationary phase approximation
c. Bounded function
d. Derivative

8. The function difference divided by the point difference is known as the _____, it is also known as Newton's quotient):

$$\frac{\Delta F(P)}{\Delta P} = \frac{F(P + \Delta P) - F(P)}{\Delta P} = \frac{\nabla F(P + \Delta P)}{\Delta P}.$$

If ΔP is infinitesimal, then the _____ is a derivative, otherwise it is a divided difference:

$$\text{If } |\Delta P| = iota: \quad \frac{\Delta F(P)}{\Delta P} = \frac{dF(P)}{dP} = F'(P) = G(P);$$

$$\text{If } |\Delta P| > iota: \quad \frac{\Delta F(P)}{\Delta P} = \frac{DF(P)}{DP} = F[P, P + \Delta P].$$

Regardless if ΔP is infinitesimal or finite, there is (at least--in the case of the derivative--theoretically) a point range, where the boundaries are P ± (.5)ΔP (depending on the orientation--ΔF(P), δF(P) or ∇F(P)):

LB = Lower Boundary; UB = Upper Boundary;

Chapter 2. KEY CONCEPT: THE DERIVATIVE

Anyone familiar with derivatives knows that they can be regarded as functions themselves, harboring their own derivatives. Thus each function is home to sequential degrees ('higher orders') of derivation, or differentiation. This property can be generalized to all difference quotients. As this sequencing requires a corresponding boundary splintering, it is practical to break up the point range into smaller, equi-sized sections, with each section being marked by an intermediary point ('P_i'), where LB = P_0 and UB = P_{A_n}, the nth point, equaling the degree/order:

LB = P_0 = P_0 + $0\Delta_1 P$ = P_{A_n} - $(Åf-0)\Delta_1 P$; P_1 = P_0 + $1\Delta_1 P$ = P_{A_n} - $(Åf-1)\Delta_1 P$; P_2 = P_0 + $2\Delta_1 P$ = P_{A_n} - $(Åf-2)\Delta_1 P$; P_3 = P_0 + $3\Delta_1 P$ = P_{A_n} - $(Åf-3)\Delta_1 P$; ↓↓↓↓ P_{A_n-3} = P_0 + $(Åf-3)\Delta_1 P$ = P_{A_n} - $3\Delta_1 P$; P_{A_n-2} = P_0 + $(Åf-2)\Delta_1 P$ = P_{A_n} - $2\Delta_1 P$; P_{A_n-1} = P_0 + $(Åf-1)\Delta_1 P$ = P_{A_n} - $1\Delta_1 P$; UB = P_{A_n-0} = P_0 + $(Åf-0)\Delta_1 P$ = P_{A_n} - $0\Delta_1 P$ = P_{A_n};

$\Delta P = \Delta_1 P = P_1 - P_0 = P_2 - P_1 = P_3 - P_2 = \ldots$

a. Notation for differentiation
b. Continuously differentiable
c. Directional derivative
d. Difference quotient

9. In geometry, the _____ (or simply the tangent) to a curve at a given point is the straight line that 'just touches' the curve at that point (in the sense explained more precisely below.) As it passes through the point of tangency, the _____ is 'going in the same direction' as the curve, and in this sense it is the best straight-line approximation to the curve at that point. The same definition applies to space curves and curves in n-dimensional Euclidean space.

a. Lie derivative
b. Minimal surface
c. North pole
d. Tangent line

10. f'(x) is twice the absolute value function, and it does not have a derivative at zero. Similar examples show that a function can have k derivatives for any non-negative integer k but no (k + 1)-order derivative. A function that has k successive derivatives is called _____.

a. Power series
b. K times differentiable
c. Differential coefficient
d. Differential calculus

11. In mathematics, a _____ is a function which preserves the given order. This concept first arose in calculus, and was later generalized to the more abstract setting of order theory.

In calculus, a function f defined on a subset of the real numbers with real values is called monotonic (also monotonically increasing or non-decreasing), if for all x and y such that x >≤ y one has f(x) >≤ f(y), so f preserves the order.

a. Monotonic function
b. Pseudo-differential operator
c. Pettis integral
d. 15 theorem

12. This article will state and prove the _____ for differentiation, and then use it to prove these two formulas.

The _____ for differentiation states that for every natural number n, the derivative of $f(x) = x^n$ is $f'(x) = nx^{n-1}$, that is,

$$(x^n)' = nx^{n-1}.$$

The _____ for integration

$$\int x^n \, dx = \frac{x^{n+1}}{n+1} + C$$

for natural n is then an easy consequence. One just needs to take the derivative of this equality and use the _____ and linearity of differentiation on the right-hand side.

a. Power rule
b. Test for Divergence
c. Leibniz rule
d. Functional integration

13. If a function has an integral, it is said to be integrable. The function for which the integral is calculated is called the _____. The region over which a function is being integrated is called the domain of integration.

a. Integrand
b. Integration by parts
c. Order of integration
d. Integral test for convergence

14. Let f be a differentiable function, and let f'(x) be its derivative. The derivative of f'(x) (if it has one) is written f''(x) and is called the _____ of f. Similarly, the derivative of a _____, if it exists, is written f'''(x) and is called the third derivative of f.

a. Vertical asymptote
b. Second derivative
c. Slant asymptote
d. Stationary phase approximation

15. The _____ is a polynomial mapping of degree 2, often cited as an archetypal example of how complex, chaotic behaviour can arise from very simple non-linear dynamical equations. The map was popularized in a seminal 1976 paper by the biologist Robert May, in part as a discrete-time demographic model analogous to the logistic equation first created by Pierre François Verhulst. Mathematically, the _____ is written

$$(1) \quad x_{n+1} = r x_n (1 - x_n)$$

where:

x_n is a number between zero and one, and represents the population at year n, and hence x_0 represents the initial population (at year 0)

r is a positive number, and represents a combined rate for reproduction and starvation.

a. 15 theorem
b. Logistic map
c. BIBO stability
d. BDDC

16. In physics, and more specifically kinematics, _____ is the change in velocity over time. Because velocity is a vector, it can change in two ways: a change in magnitude and/or a change in direction. In one dimension, _____ is the rate at which something speeds up or slows down.
   a. ACTRAN
   b. Acceleration
   c. ALGOR
   d. AUSM

17. In mathematics, a _____ represents the application of one function to the results of another. For instance, the functions f: X → Y and g: Y → Z can be composed by first computing f(x) and then applying a function g to the output of f(x).

Thus one obtains a function g ∘ f: X → Z defined by (g ∘ f)(x) = g(f(x)) for all x in X. The notation g ∘ f is read as 'g circle f', or 'g composed with f', 'g after f', 'g following f', or just 'g of f'.

   a. Surjective
   b. Piecewise-defined function
   c. Composite function
   d. Constant function

18. In mathematics, the _____ (or modulus) of a real number is its numerical value without regard to its sign. So, for example, 3 is the _____ of both 3 and −3.

The _____ of a number a is denoted by | a |.

   a. Area hyperbolic functions
   b. Exponential function
   c. Absolute value
   d. ACTRAN

19. The _____, L, of a dynamical system is a function that summarizes the dynamics of the system. It is named after Joseph Louis Lagrange. The concept of a _____ was originally introduced in a reformulation of classical mechanics known as _____ mechanics.
   a. Vector potential
   b. Klein-Gordon equation
   c. Dirac equation
   d. Lagrangian

20. In mathematics, a _____ is a function whose definition is dependent on the value of the independent variable. Mathematically, a real-valued function f of a real variable x is a relationship whose definition is given differently on disjoint subsets of its domain

The word piecewise is also used to describe any property of a _____ that holds for each piece but may not hold for the whole domain of the function.

   a. Constant function
   b. Piecewise-defined function
   c. Surjective
   d. Range

21. In mathematics, a _____ is a piecewise-defined function whose pieces are linear. For example, the function

$$f(x) = \begin{cases} -x - 3 & \text{if } x \leq -3 \\ x + 3 & \text{if } -3 < x \leq 0 \\ 3 - 2x & \text{if } 0 \leq x < 3 \\ x - 3 & \text{if } x \geq 3 \end{cases}$$

is piecewise linear with four pieces. (The graph of this function is shown to the right.)

a. 15 theorem
b. Non-Newtonian calculus
c. Piecewise linear function
d. Multiplicative calculus

22. A _____ is the difference between the calculated approximation of a number and its exact mathematical value. Numerical analysis specifically tries to estimate this error when using approximation equations and/or algorithms, especially when using finite digits to represent infinite digits of real numbers. This is a form of quantization error.
a. Round-off error
b. BIBO stability
c. 15 theorem
d. BDDC

Chapter 3. SHORT-CUTS TO DIFFERENTIATION

1. The _____ is a function in mathematics. The application of this function to a value x is written as exp(x). Equivalently, this can be written in the form e^x, where e is a mathematical constant, the base of the natural logarithm, which equals approximately 2.718281828, and is also known as Euler's number.
   - a. Area hyperbolic functions
   - b. ACTRAN
   - c. Exponential function
   - d. Integral part

2. In calculus, a branch of mathematics, the _____ is a measurement of how a function changes when its input changes. Loosely speaking, a _____ can be thought of as how much a quantity is changing at some given point. For example, the _____ of the position (or distance) of a vehicle with respect to time is the instantaneous velocity (respectively, instantaneous speed) at which the vehicle is traveling.

   The process of finding a _____ is called differentiation. The fundamental theorem of calculus states that differentiation is the reverse process to integration.
   - a. Semi-differentiability
   - b. Stationary phase approximation
   - c. Bounded function
   - d. Derivative

3. A _____ is the difference between the calculated approximation of a number and its exact mathematical value. Numerical analysis specifically tries to estimate this error when using approximation equations and/or algorithms, especially when using finite digits to represent infinite digits of real numbers. This is a form of quantization error.
   - a. BIBO stability
   - b. BDDC
   - c. 15 theorem
   - d. Round-off error

4. In mathematics, the concept of a '_____' is used to describe the behavior of a function as its argument or input either 'gets close' to some point, or as the argument becomes arbitrarily large; or the behavior of a sequence's elements as their index increases indefinitely. Limits are used in calculus and other branches of mathematical analysis to define derivatives and continuity.

   In formulas, _____ is usually abbreviated as lim
   - a. BIBO stability
   - b. BDDC
   - c. 15 theorem
   - d. Limit

5. In the two-dimensional case, a _____ perpendicularly intersects the tangent line to a curve at a given point.

   The _____ is often used in computer graphics to determine a surface's orientation toward a light source for flat shading, or the orientation of each of the corners (vertices) to mimic a curved surface with Phong shading.

   For a polygon (such as a triangle), a surface normal can be calculated as the vector cross product of two (non-parallel) edges of the polygon.
   - a. Hyperbolic paraboloid
   - b. Parametric surface
   - c. PDE surfaces
   - d. Normal line

6. In calculus, the _____ is a formula used to find the derivatives of products of functions. It may be stated thus:

Chapter 3. SHORT-CUTS TO DIFFERENTIATION

$$(f \cdot g)' = f' \cdot g + f \cdot g'$$

or in the Leibniz notation thus:

$$\frac{d}{dx}(u \cdot v) = u \cdot \frac{dv}{dx} + v \cdot \frac{du}{dx}.$$

Discovery of this rule is credited to Gottfried Leibniz, who demonstrated it using differentials. Here is Leibniz's argument: Let u and v be two differentiable functions of x.

a. Quotient Rule
c. Constant factor rule in differentiation
b. Differentiation rules
d. Product rule

7. In calculus, the _____ is a method of finding the derivative of a function that is the quotient of two other functions for which derivatives exist.

If the function one wishes to differentiate, f(x), can be written as

$$f(x) = \frac{g(x)}{h(x)}$$

and h(x) ≠ 0, then the rule states that the derivative of g(x) / h(x) is equal to:

$$\frac{d}{dx}f(x) = f'(x) = \frac{g'(x)h(x) - g(x)h'(x)}{[h(x)]^2}.$$

Or, more precisely, if all x in some open set containing the number a satisfy h(x) ≠ 0; and g'(a) and h'(a) both exist; then, f'(a) exists as well and:

$$f'(a) = \frac{g'(a)h(a) - g(a)h'(a)}{[h(a)]^2}.$$

The derivative of (4x − 2) / (x² + 1) is:

$$\frac{d}{dx}\left[\frac{(4x-2)}{x^2+1}\right] = \frac{(x^2+1)(4) - (4x-2)(2x)}{(x^2+1)^2}$$

$$= \frac{(4x^2+4) - (8x^2-4x)}{(x^2+1)^2} = \frac{-4x^2+4x+4}{(x^2+1)^2}$$

In the example above, the choices

g(x) = 4x − 2
h(x) = x² + 1

were made. Analogously, the derivative of sin(x) / x² (when x ≠ 0) is:

$$\frac{\cos(x)x^2 - \sin(x)2x}{x^4}$$

Another example is:

$$f(x) = \frac{2x^2}{x^3}$$

whereas g(x) = 2x² and h(x) = x³, and g'(x) = 4x and h'(x) = 3x².

    a. Differentiation rules   b. Reciprocal Rule
    c. Constant factor rule in differentiation   d. Quotient rule

8. In a totally ordered set all elements are mutually comparable, so such a set can have at most one minimal element and at most one maximal element. Then, due to mutual comparability, the minimal element will also be the least element and the maximal element will also be the greatest element. Thus in a totally ordered set we can simply use the terms minimum and _____.

    a. Leibniz rule   b. Nth term
    c. Racetrack principle   d. Maximum

9. In calculus, the _____ is a formula for the derivative of the composite of two functions.

In intuitive terms, if a variable, y, depends on a second variable, u, which in turn depends on a third variable, x, then the rate of change of y with respect to x can be computed as the rate of change of y with respect to u multiplied by the rate of change of u with respect to x. Schematically,

$$\frac{dy}{dx} = \frac{dy}{du} \cdot \frac{du}{dx}.$$

    a. Chain rule   b. Product rule
    c. Differentiation rules   d. Reciprocal Rule

10. In mathematics, a _____ represents the application of one function to the results of another. For instance, the functions f: X → Y and g: Y → Z can be composed by first computing f(x) and then applying a function g to the output of f(x.)

Thus one obtains a function g ∘ f: X → Z defined by (g ∘ f)(x) = g(f(x)) for all x in X. The notation g ∘ f is read as 'g circle f', or 'g composed with f', 'g after f', 'g following f', or just 'g of f'.

    a. Composite function   b. Surjective
    c. Constant function   d. Piecewise-defined function

11. A quantity is said to be subject to _____ if it decreases at a rate proportional to its value. Symbolically, this can be expressed as the following differential equation, where N is the quantity and λ is a positive number called the decay constant.

$$\frac{dN}{dt} = -\lambda N.$$

The solution to this equation is:

$$N(t) = N_0 e^{-\lambda t}.$$

Here N(t) is the quantity at time t, and N_0 = N(0) is the initial quantity, i.e. the quantity at time t = 0.

a. Exponential sum
b. ACTRAN
c. ALGOR
d. Exponential decay

12. The _____ of an angle is the ratio of the length of the opposite side to the length of the hypotenuse. In our case

$$\sin A = \frac{\text{opposite}}{\text{hypotenuse}} = \frac{a}{h}.$$

Note that this ratio does not depend on size of the particular right triangle chosen, as long as it contains the angle A, since all such triangles are similar.

The cosine of an angle is the ratio of the length of the adjacent side to the length of the hypotenuse.

a. Sine integral
b. Trigonometric
c. Trigonometric functions
d. Sine

13. Trigonometry is a branch of mathematics that deals with triangles, particularly those plane triangles in which one angle has 90 degrees (right triangles.) Trigonometry deals with relationships between the sides and the angles of triangles and with the _____ functions, which describe those relationships.

Trigonometry has applications in both pure mathematics and in applied mathematics, where it is essential in many branches of science and technology.

a. Trigonometric functions
b. Sine
c. Trigonometric integrals
d. Trigonometric

14. In mathematics, the _____ are functions of an angle. They are important in the study of triangles and modeling periodic phenomena, among many other applications. _____ are commonly defined as ratios of two sides of a right triangle containing the angle, and can equivalently be defined as the lengths of various line segments from a unit circle.

Chapter 3. SHORT-CUTS TO DIFFERENTIATION

a. Trigonometric integrals
b. Sine integral
c. Trigonometric
d. Trigonometric functions

15. In geometry, the _____ (or simply the tangent) to a curve at a given point is the straight line that 'just touches' the curve at that point (in the sense explained more precisely below.) As it passes through the point of tangency, the _____ is 'going in the same direction' as the curve, and in this sense it is the best straight-line approximation to the curve at that point. The same definition applies to space curves and curves in n-dimensional Euclidean space.

a. Lie derivative
b. Minimal surface
c. North pole
d. Tangent line

16. The most commonly encountered form of Hooke's law is probably the spring equation, which relates the force exerted by a spring to the distance it is stretched by a _____, k, measured in force per length.

$$F = -kx$$

The negative sign indicates that the force exerted by the spring is in direct opposition to the direction of displacement. It is called a 'restoring force', as it tends to restore the system to equilibrium.

a. Spring equation
b. Navier-Stokes equations
c. Polar moment of inertia
d. Spring constant

17. The function $\log_b(x)$ depends on both b and x, but the term _____ in standard usage refers to a function of the form $\log_b(x)$ in which the base b is fixed and so the only argument is x. Thus there is one _____ for each value of the base b (which must be positive and must differ from 1.) Viewed in this way, the base-b _____ is the inverse function of the exponential function b^x.

a. Logarithm function
b. BDDC
c. 15 theorem
d. BIBO stability

18. In mathematics, the _____ of a function y = f(x) is a function that, in some fashion, 'undoes' the effect of f. The _____ of f is denoted f^{-1}. The statements y=f(x) and x=f^{-1}(y) are equivalent.

a. ACTRAN
b. AUSM
c. Inverse
d. ALGOR

19. In mathematics, the _____ or cyclometric functions are the inverse functions of the trigonometric functions. The principal inverses are listed in the following table.

If x is allowed to be a complex number, then the range of y applies only to its real part.

a. ALGOR
b. AUSM
c. ACTRAN
d. Inverse trigonometric functions

20.

In differential calculus, _____ problems involve finding a rate that a quantity changes by relating the population of the earth. The rate of change is usually with respect to people who have died.

Chapter 3. SHORT-CUTS TO DIFFERENTIATION

a. Mean Value Theorem
b. Visual Calculus
c. Standard part function
d. Related rates

21. In physics, and more specifically kinematics, _____ is the change in velocity over time. Because velocity is a vector, it can change in two ways: a change in magnitude and/or a change in direction. In one dimension, _____ is the rate at which something speeds up or slows down.
   a. ALGOR
   b. Acceleration
   c. AUSM
   d. ACTRAN

22. In calculus, a method called _____ can be applied to implicitly defined functions. This method is an application of the chain rule allowing one to calculate the derivative of a function given implicitly.

As explained in the introduction, y can be given as a function of x implicitly rather than explicitly. When we have an equation R (x,y) = 0, we may be able to solve it for y and then differentiate. However, sometimes it is simpler to differentiate R(x,y) with respect to x and then solve for dy / dx.

   a. Automatic differentiation
   b. Ordinary differential equation
   c. Implicit function
   d. Implicit differentiation

23. In mathematics, an _____ is a generalization for the concept of a function in which the dependent variable has not been given 'explicitly' in terms of the independent variable. To give a function f explicitly is to provide a prescription for determining the output value of the function y in terms of the input value x:

   y = f(x.)

By contrast, the function is implicit if the value of y is obtained from x by solving an equation of the form:

   R(x,y) = 0.

   a. Ordinary differential equation
   b. Automatic differentiation
   c. Implicit differentiation
   d. Implicit function

24. In infinitesimal calculus, a _____ is traditionally an infinitesimally small change in a variable. For example, if x is a variable, then a change in the value of x is often denoted Δx (or δx when this change is considered to be small.) The _____ dx represents such a change, but is infinitely small.
   a. Differential
   b. Dirichlet integral
   c. The Method of Mechanical Theorems
   d. Local maximum

25. A _____ is a mathematical equation for an unknown function of one or several variables that relates the values of the function itself and of its derivatives of various orders. they play a prominent role in engineering, physics, economics and other disciplines.

A simplified real world example of a _____ is modeling the acceleration of a ball falling through the air (considering only gravity and air resistance.)

a. Structural stability
b. Caloric polynomial
c. Phase line
d. Differential equation

26. In mathematics, _____ are a method of defining a curve. A simple kinematical example is when one uses a time parameter to determine the position, velocity, and other information about a body in motion.

Abstractly, a relation is given in the form of an equation, and it is shown also to be the image of functions from items such as R^n.

a. Partial derivative
b. Parametric equations
c. Shift theorem
d. Critical point

27. In physics, _____ is defined as the rate of change of position. it is vector physical quantity; both speed and direction are required to define it. In the SI (metric) system, it is measured in meters per second: (m/s) or ms^{-1}.
a. BIBO stability
b. BDDC
c. Velocity
d. 15 theorem

28. In mathematics, a (topological) _____ is defined as follows: let I be an interval of real numbers (i.e. a non-empty connected subset of $\mathbb{R}$); then a _____ γ is a continuous mapping $\gamma : I \to X$, where X is a topological space. The _____ γ is said to be simple if it is injective, i.e. if for all x, y in I, we have $\gamma(x) = \gamma(y) \implies x = y$. If I is a closed bounded interval $[a, b]$, we also allow the possibility $\gamma(a) = \gamma(b)$ (this convention makes it possible to talk about closed simple _____.)

a. Prolate cycloid
b. Tractrix
c. Closed curve
d. Curve

29. In mathematics, a _____ is the graph of the system of parametric equations

$$x = A\sin(at + \delta), \quad y = B\sin(bt),$$

which describes complex harmonic motion. This family of curves was investigated by Nathaniel Bowditch in 1815, and later in more detail by Jules Antoine Lissajous in 1857.

The appearance of the figure is highly sensitive to the ratio a/b.

a. Lissajous curve
b. BDDC
c. 15 theorem
d. BIBO stability

30. In mathematics, a _____ is an approximation of a general function using a linear function (more precisely, an affine function.)

Given a differentiable function f of one real variable, Taylor's theorem for n=1 states that

$$f(x) = f(a) + f'(a)(x-a) + R_2$$

where R_2 is the remainder term. The _____ is obtained by dropping the remainder:

$$f(x) \approx f(a) + f'(a)(x-a)$$

which is true for x close to a.

a. Linear approximation
c. Smooth function
b. Point of inflection
d. Lin-Tsien equation

31. In mathematics and its applications, _____ refers to finding the linear approximation to a function at a given point. In the study of dynamical systems, _____ is a method for assessing the local stability of an equilibrium point of a system of nonlinear differential equations or discrete dynamical systems. This method is used in fields such as engineering, physics, economics, and ecology.

a. Smooth function
c. Differentiation of trigonometric functions
b. Linearization
d. Parametric derivative

32. The _____ in some data is the discrepancy between an exact value and some approximation to it. An _____ can occur because

1. the measurement of the data is not precise (due to the instruments), or
2. approximations are used instead of the real data (e.g., 3.14 instead of π.)

In the mathematical field of numerical analysis, the numerical stability of an algorithm in numerical analysis indicates how the error is propagated by the algorithm.

One commonly distinguishes between the relative error and the absolute error. The absolute error is the magnitude of the difference between the exact value and the approximation.

a. AUSM
c. ACTRAN
b. ALGOR
d. Approximation error

33. f'(x) is twice the absolute value function, and it does not have a derivative at zero. Similar examples show that a function can have k derivatives for any non-negative integer k but no (k + 1)-order derivative. A function that has k successive derivatives is called _____.

a. K times differentiable
c. Differential calculus
b. Differential coefficient
d. Power series

Chapter 4. USING THE DERIVATIVE

1. In mathematics, a _____ is a function which preserves the given order. This concept first arose in calculus, and was later generalized to the more abstract setting of order theory.

   In calculus, a function f defined on a subset of the real numbers with real values is called monotonic (also monotonically increasing or non-decreasing), if for all x and y such that x >≤ y one has f(x) >≤ f(y), so f preserves the order.

   a. Pseudo-differential operator
   b. Pettis integral
   c. 15 theorem
   d. Monotonic function

2. In calculus, a branch of mathematics, the _____ is a measurement of how a function changes when its input changes. Loosely speaking, a _____ can be thought of as how much a quantity is changing at some given point. For example, the _____ of the position (or distance) of a vehicle with respect to time is the instantaneous velocity (respectively, instantaneous speed) at which the vehicle is traveling.

   The process of finding a _____ is called differentiation. The fundamental theorem of calculus states that differentiation is the reverse process to integration.

   a. Derivative
   b. Semi-differentiability
   c. Stationary phase approximation
   d. Bounded function

3. A _____ is the difference between the calculated approximation of a number and its exact mathematical value. Numerical analysis specifically tries to estimate this error when using approximation equations and/or algorithms, especially when using finite digits to represent infinite digits of real numbers. This is a form of quantization error.

   a. 15 theorem
   b. BDDC
   c. BIBO stability
   d. Round-off error

4. In mathematics, a _____ (or critical number) is a point on the domain of a function where:

   - one dimension: the derivative (or slope of the line when visualized) is equal to zero or a point where the function ceases to be differentiable.
   - in general: there are two distinct concepts: either the derivative (Jacobian) vanishes, or it is not of full rank (or, in either case, the function is not differentiable); these agree in one dimension.

   Note that in one dimension, a critical value or critical number x of function f is the domain element at which the derivative is zero or undefined, whereas the associated ordered pair (x, y) is the _____. In higher dimensions a critical value is in the range whereas a _____ is in the domain.

   There are two situations in which a point becomes a _____ of a function of one variable. The first of which is that the value of the first derivative is equal to zero.

   a. Differentiation operator
   b. Critical point
   c. Total derivative
   d. Multivariable calculus

5. In differential topology, a _____ of a differentiable function between differentiable manifolds is the image of a critical point.

Chapter 4. USING THE DERIVATIVE

The basic result on critical values is Sard's lemma. The set of critical values can be quite irregular; but in Morse theory it becomes important to consider real-valued functions on a manifold M, such that the set of critical values is in fact finite.

a. Critical value
b. P-Laplacian
c. Disk algebra
d. Solenoidal

6. In mathematics, _____ and minima, known collectively as extrema, are the largest value (maximum) or smallest value (minimum), that a function takes in a point either within a given neighbourhood (local extremum) or on the function domain in its entirety (global extremum.)

Throughout, a point refers to an input (x), while a value refers to an output (y): one distinguishing between the maximum value and the point (or points) at which it occurs.

A real-valued function f defined on the real line is said to have a local maximum point at the point x^*, if there exists some $\varepsilon > 0$, such that $f(x^*) \geq f(x)$ when $|x - x^*| < \varepsilon$.

a. Leibniz formula
b. Racetrack principle
c. Related rates
d. Maxima

7. In calculus, the _____ determines whether a given critical point of a function is a maximum, a minimum, or neither.

Suppose that f is a function and we want to determine if f has a maximum or minimum at x. If f is increasing to the left of x and decreasing to the right of x, then x is a local maximum of f.

a. Test for Divergence
b. Partial sum
c. Continuous function
d. First derivative test

8. In differential calculus, an inflection point, or _____ (or inflexion) is a point on a curve at which the curvature changes sign. The curve changes from being concave upwards (positive curvature) to concave downwards (negative curvature), or vice versa. If one imagines driving a vehicle along the curve, it is a point at which the steering-wheel is momentarily 'straight', being turned from left to right or vice versa.

a. Lin-Tsien equation
b. Logarithmic derivative
c. Derivative of a constant
d. Point of inflection

9. Let f be a differentiable function, and let f'(x) be its derivative. The derivative of f'(x) (if it has one) is written f''(x) and is called the _____ of f. Similarly, the derivative of a _____, if it exists, is written f'''(x) and is called the third derivative of f.

a. Vertical asymptote
b. Stationary phase approximation
c. Slant asymptote
d. Second derivative

10. In calculus, a branch of mathematics, the _____ is a criterion often useful for determining whether a given stationary point of a function is a local maximum or a local minimum.

The test states: If the function f is twice differentiable at a stationary point x, meaning that $f'(x)=0$, then:

- If $f''(x)<0$ then f has a local maximum at x.
- If $f''(x)>0$ then f has a local minimum at x.
- If $f''(x)=0$, the _____ says nothing about the point x, has a possible inflection point.

In the last case, the function may have a local maximum or minimum there, but the function is sufficiently 'flat' that this is undetected by the second derivative. In this case one has to examine the third derivative. Such an example is f(x) = x⁴.

a. Second derivative test
b. Stationary point
c. Linearity of differentiation
d. Symmetric derivative

11. In economics, the _____ functional form of production functions is widely used to represent the relationship of an output to inputs. It was proposed by Knut Wicksell (1851-1926), and tested against statistical evidence by Charles Cobb and Paul Douglas in 1900-1928.

For production, the function is

Y = AL^α K^β,

where:

- Y = total production (the monetary value of all goods produced in a year)
- L = labor input
- K = capital input
- A = total factor productivity
- α and β are the output elasticities of labor and capital, respectively. These values are constants determined by available technology.

Output elasticity measures the responsiveness of output to a change in levels of either labor or capital used in production, ceteris paribus. For example if α = 0.15, a 1% increase in labor would lead to approximately a 0.15% increase in output.

a. 15 theorem
b. BDDC
c. BIBO stability
d. Cobb-Douglas

12. In integral calculus we would want to write a fractional algebraic expression as the sum of its _____ in order to take the integral of each simple fraction separately. Once the original denominator, D_0, has been factored we set up a fraction for each factor in the denominator. We may use a subscripted D to represent the denominator of the respective _____ which are the factors in D_0.

Chapter 4. USING THE DERIVATIVE

a. Multinomial theorem
b. Closed-form expression
c. Left inverse
d. Partial fractions

13. The _____ is an important family of continuous probability distributions, applicable in many fields. Each member of the family may be defined by two parameters, location and scale: the mean and variance respectively. The standard _____ is the _____ with a mean of zero and a variance of one.
   a. Correlation
   b. Moment
   c. Continuous random variable
   d. Normal distribution

14. In mathematics, a (topological) _____ is defined as follows: let I be an interval of real numbers (i.e. a non-empty connected subset of $\mathbb{R}$); then a _____ γ is a continuous mapping $\gamma : I \to X$, where X is a topological space. The _____ γ is said to be simple if it is injective, i.e. if for all x, y in I, we have $\gamma(x) = \gamma(y) \implies x = y$. If I is a closed bounded interval $[a, b]$, we also allow the possibility $\gamma(a) = \gamma(b)$ (this convention makes it possible to talk about closed simple _____.)
   a. Prolate cycloid
   b. Tractrix
   c. Curve
   d. Closed curve

15. An _____ of a real-valued function y = f(x) is a curve which describes the behavior of f as either x or y tends to infinity.

In other words, as one moves along the graph of f(x) in some direction, the distance between it and the _____ eventually becomes smaller than any distance that one may specify.

   a. ALGOR
   b. ACTRAN
   c. AUSM
   d. Asymptote

16. In physics, _____ is defined as the rate of change of position. it is vector physical quantity; both speed and direction are required to define it. In the SI (metric) system, it is measured in meters per second: (m/s) or ms^{-1}.
   a. 15 theorem
   b. BDDC
   c. BIBO stability
   d. Velocity

17. The _____, L, of a dynamical system is a function that summarizes the dynamics of the system. It is named after Joseph Louis Lagrange. The concept of a _____ was originally introduced in a reformulation of classical mechanics known as _____ mechanics.
   a. Lagrangian
   b. Dirac equation
   c. Vector potential
   d. Klein-Gordon equation

18. In mathematics, the simplest case of _____ refers to the study of problems in which one seeks to minimize or maximize a real function by systematically choosing the values of real or integer variables from within an allowed set. This (a scalar real valued objective function) is actually a small subset of this field which comprises a large area of applied mathematics and generalizes to study of means to obtain 'best available' values of some objective function given a defined domain where the elaboration is on the types of functions and the conditions and nature of the objects in the problem domain.

The first _____ technique, which is known as steepest descent, goes back to Gauss.

a. ACTRAN
b. AUSM
c. Optimization
d. ALGOR

19. In mathematics, especially in order theory, an upper bound of a subset S of some partially ordered set (P, ≤) is an element of P which is greater than or equal to every element of S. The term _____ is defined dually as an element of P which is lesser than or equal to every element of S. A set with an upper bound is said to be bounded from above by that bound, a set with a _____ is said to be bounded from below by that bound.

A subset S of a partially ordered set P may fail to have any bounds or may have many different upper and lower bounds. By transitivity, any element greater than or equal to an upper bound of S is again an upper bound of S, and any element lesser than or equal to any _____ of S is again a _____ of S. This leads to the consideration of least upper bounds: (or suprema) and greatest lower bounds (or infima.)

a. Lower bound
b. BIBO stability
c. 15 theorem
d. BDDC

20. In mathematics, especially in order theory, an _____ of a subset S of some partially ordered set (P, >≤) is an element of P which is greater than or equal to every element of S. The term lower bound is defined dually as an element of P which is lesser than or equal to every element of S. A set with an _____ is said to be bounded from above by that bound, a set with a lower bound is said to be bounded from below by that bound.

A subset S of a partially ordered set P may fail to have any bounds or may have many different upper and lower bounds. By transitivity, any element greater than or equal to an _____ of S is again an _____ of S, and any element lesser than or equal to any lower bound of S is again a lower bound of S. This leads to the consideration of least upper bounds: (or suprema) and greatest lower bounds (or infima.)

a. ALGOR
b. ACTRAN
c. AUSM
d. Upper bound

21. The _____, in mathematics, is a type of mean or average, which indicates the central tendency or typical value of a set of numbers. It is similar to the arithmetic mean, which is what most people think of with the word 'average,' except that instead of adding the set of numbers and then dividing the sum by the count of numbers in the set, n, the numbers are multiplied and then the nth root of the resulting product is taken.

For instance, the _____ of two numbers, say 2 and 8, is just the square root (i.e., the second root) of their product, 16, which is 4.

a. Standard deviation
b. Continuous random variable
c. Normal distribution
d. Geometric mean

22. In probability theory and statistics, the _____ (or expectation value or mean and for continuous random variables with a density function it is the probability density -weighted integral of the possible values.

The term '_____' can be misleading.

Chapter 4. USING THE DERIVATIVE

a. ALGOR
b. AUSM
c. ACTRAN
d. Expected value

23. In physics and geometry, the _____ is the theoretical shape of a hanging flexible chain or cable when supported at its ends and acted upon by a uniform gravitational force (its own weight) and in equilibrium. The curve has a U shape that is similar in appearance to the parabola, though it is a different curve.
    a. 15 theorem
    b. BDDC
    c. BIBO stability
    d. Catenary

24. In mathematics, the hyperbolic functions are analogs of the ordinary trigonometric functions. The basic hyperbolic functions are the hyperbolic sine 'sinh', and the _____ 'cosh', from which are derived the hyperbolic tangent 'tanh', etc., in analogy to the derived trigonometric functions. The inverse hyperbolic functions are the area hyperbolic sine 'arsinh' (also called 'asinh', or sometimes by the misnomer of 'arcsinh') and so on.
    a. Hyperbolic cosine
    b. Step function
    c. Hyperbolic tangent
    d. Square root function

25. The _____ of an angle is the ratio of the length of the opposite side to the length of the hypotenuse. In our case

$$\sin A = \frac{\text{opposite}}{\text{hypotenuse}} = \frac{a}{h}.$$

Note that this ratio does not depend on size of the particular right triangle chosen, as long as it contains the angle A, since all such triangles are similar.

The cosine of an angle is the ratio of the length of the adjacent side to the length of the hypotenuse.

   a. Trigonometric
   b. Sine integral
   c. Sine
   d. Trigonometric functions

26. In geometry, the _____ (or simply the tangent) to a curve at a given point is the straight line that 'just touches' the curve at that point (in the sense explained more precisely below.) As it passes through the point of tangency, the _____ is 'going in the same direction' as the curve, and in this sense it is the best straight-line approximation to the curve at that point. The same definition applies to space curves and curves in n-dimensional Euclidean space.
    a. Tangent line
    b. Lie derivative
    c. North pole
    d. Minimal surface

27. The largest and the smallest element of a set are called extreme values, absolute extrema, or extreme records.

For a differentiable function f, if $f(x_0)$ is an _____ for the set of all values f(x), and if x_0 is in the interior of the domain of f, then x_0 is a critical point, by Fermat's theorem.

In the case of a general partial order one should not confuse a least element (smaller than all other) and a minimal element (nothing is smaller.)

a. Extreme Value Theorem
b. Infinitesimal
c. Integration by substitution
d. Extreme Value

28. In calculus, the _____ states that if a real-valued function f is continuous in the closed and bounded interval [a,b], then f must attain its maximum and minimum value, each at least once. That is, there exist numbers c and d in [a,b] such that:

$$f(c) \geq f(x) \geq f(d) \quad \text{for all } x \in [a, b].$$

A related theorem is the boundedness theorem which states that a continuous function f in the closed interval [a,b] is bounded on that interval. That is, there exist real numbers m and M such that:

$$m \leq f(x) \leq M \quad \text{for all } x \in [a, b].$$

The _____ enriches the boundedness theorem by saying that not only is the function bounded, but it also attains its least upper bound as its maximum and its greatest lower bound as its minimum.

a. Uniform convergence
b. Extreme Value Theorem
c. Integral of secant cubed
d. Infinitesimal

29. In calculus, the _____ states, roughly, that given a section of a smooth curve, there is at least one point on that section at which the derivative (slope) of the curve is equal (parallel) to the 'average' derivative of the section. It is used to prove theorems that make global conclusions about a function on an interval starting from local hypotheses about derivatives at points of the interval.

This theorem can be understood concretely by applying it to motion: If a car travels one hundred miles in one hour, so its average speed during that time was 100 miles per hour.

a. Limits of integration
b. Periodic function
c. Hyperbolic angle
d. Mean Value Theorem

30. In mathematics, a _____ is a function whose values do not vary and thus are constant. For example, if we have the function f(x) = 4, then f is constant since f maps any value to 4. More formally, a function f : A → B is a _____ if f(x) = f(y) for all x and y in A.

a. Range
b. Surjective
c. Piecewise-defined function
d. Constant Function

31. In calculus, the _____ describes the movement and growth of two functions in terms of their derivatives.

This principle is derived from the fact that if a horse named Franky Fleetfeet always runs faster than a horse named Greg Gooseleg, then if Frank and Greg start a race from the same place and the same time, then Frank will win. More briefly, the horse that starts fast and stays fast wins.

a. Maximum
b. Periodic function
c. Test for Divergence
d. Racetrack Principle

Chapter 5. KEY CONCEPT: THE DEFINITE INTEGRAL

1. Cantor defined two kinds of _____ numbers, the ordinal numbers and the cardinal numbers. Ordinal numbers may be identified with well-ordered sets, or counting carried on to any stopping point, including points after an _____ number have already been counted. Generalizing finite and the ordinary _____ sequences which are maps from the positive integers leads to mappings from ordinal numbers, and transfinite sequences.

   a. ALGOR
   b. ACTRAN
   c. AUSM
   d. Infinite

2. In mathematics, a _____ is a function which preserves the given order. This concept first arose in calculus, and was later generalized to the more abstract setting of order theory.

   In calculus, a function f defined on a subset of the real numbers with real values is called monotonic (also monotonically increasing or non-decreasing), if for all x and y such that x >≤ y one has f(x) >≤ f(y), so f preserves the order.

   a. Pseudo-differential operator
   b. 15 theorem
   c. Pettis integral
   d. Monotonic function

3. Integration is an important concept in mathematics, specifically in the field of calculus and, more broadly, mathematical analysis. Given a function f of a real variable x and an interval [a, b] of the real line, the _____

$$\int_a^b f(x)\,dx,$$

   is defined informally to be the net signed area of the region in the xy-plane bounded by the graph of f, the x-axis, and the vertical lines x = a and x = b.

   The term '_____' may also refer to the notion of antiderivative, a function F whose derivative is the given function f.

   a. Integrand
   b. Indefinite integral
   c. Integral
   d. Integral test for convergence

4. In mathematics, the concept of a '_____' is used to describe the behavior of a function as its argument or input either 'gets close' to some point, or as the argument becomes arbitrarily large; or the behavior of a sequence's elements as their index increases indefinitely. Limits are used in calculus and other branches of mathematical analysis to define derivatives and continuity.

   In formulas, _____ is usually abbreviated as lim

   a. BIBO stability
   b. Limit
   c. 15 theorem
   d. BDDC

5. _____ is the addition of a set of numbers; the result is their sum or total. An interim or present total of a _____ process is termed the running total. The 'numbers' to be summed may be natural numbers, complex numbers, matrices, or still more complicated objects.

a. 15 theorem b. Summation
c. BIBO stability d. BDDC

6. If a function has an integral, it is said to be integrable. The function for which the integral is calculated is called the _____. The region over which a function is being integrated is called the domain of integration.
a. Integral test for convergence b. Integration by parts
c. Order of integration d. Integrand

7. In calculus and mathematical analysis the _____ of the integral

$$\int_a^b f(x)\,dx$$

of a Riemann integrable function f defined on a closed and bounded interval [a, b] are the real numbers a and b.

_____ can also be defined for improper integrals, with the _____ of both

$$\lim_{z \to a^+} \int_z^b f(x)\,dx$$

and

$$\lim_{z \to b^-} \int_a^z f(x)\,dx$$

again being a and b. For an improper integral

$$\int_a^\infty f(x)\,dx$$

or

$$\int_{-\infty}^b f(x)\,dx$$

the _____ are a and ∞, or −∞ and b, respectively.

a. Maxima b. Differential
c. Limits of integration d. Test for Divergence

8. In mathematics, a _____ is a method for approximating the total area underneath a curve on a graph, otherwise known as an integral. It may also be used to define the integration operation.

Chapter 5. KEY CONCEPT: THE DEFINITE INTEGRAL

Consider a function $f: D \to R$, where D is a subset of the real numbers R, and let $I = [a, b]$ be a closed interval contained in D. A finite set of points $\{x_0, x_1, x_2, ... x_n\}$ such that $a = x_0 < x_1 < x_2 ... < x_n = b$ creates a partition

$$P = \{[x_0, x_1), [x_1, x_2), ... [x_{n-1}, x_n]\}$$

of I.

- a. Signed measure
- b. Solid of revolution
- c. Riemann sum
- d. Risch algorithm

9. In mathematics and its applications, a _____ system is a system for assigning an n-tuple of numbers or scalars to each point in an n-dimensional space. This concept is part of the theory of manifolds. 'Scalars' in many cases means real numbers, but, depending on context, can mean complex numbers or elements of some other commutative ring.
   - a. 15 theorem
   - b. Coordinate
   - c. Spherical coordinate system
   - d. Cylindrical coordinate system

10. The _____ specifies the relationship between the two central operations of calculus, differentiation and integration.

The first part of the theorem, sometimes called the first _____, shows that an indefinite integration can be reversed by a differentiation.

The second part, sometimes called the second _____, allows one to compute the definite integral of a function by using any one of its infinitely many antiderivatives.

- a. Periodic function
- b. Limits of integration
- c. Leibniz formula
- d. Fundamental Theorem of Calculus

11. In calculus, a branch of mathematics, the _____ is a measurement of how a function changes when its input changes. Loosely speaking, a _____ can be thought of as how much a quantity is changing at some given point. For example, the _____ of the position (or distance) of a vehicle with respect to time is the instantaneous velocity (respectively, instantaneous speed) at which the vehicle is traveling.

The process of finding a _____ is called differentiation. The fundamental theorem of calculus states that differentiation is the reverse process to integration.

- a. Semi-differentiability
- b. Derivative
- c. Stationary phase approximation
- d. Bounded function

12. The _____ is an important family of continuous probability distributions, applicable in many fields. Each member of the family may be defined by two parameters, location and scale: the mean and variance respectively. The standard _____ is the _____ with a mean of zero and a variance of one.

a. Correlation
b. Continuous random variable
c. Moment
d. Normal distribution

13. In mathematics, a (topological) _____ is defined as follows: let I be an interval of real numbers (i.e. a non-empty connected subset of $\mathbb{R}$); then a _____ γ is a continuous mapping $\gamma : I \to X$, where X is a topological space. The _____ γ is said to be simple if it is injective, i.e. if for all x, y in I, we have $\gamma(x) = \gamma(y) \implies x = y$. If I is a closed bounded interval $[a, b]$, we also allow the possibility $\gamma(a) = \gamma(b)$ (this convention makes it possible to talk about closed simple _____.)

a. Curve
b. Tractrix
c. Closed curve
d. Prolate cycloid

Chapter 6. CONSTRUCTING ANTIDERIVATIVES

1. In calculus, an _____, primitive or indefinite integral of a function f is a function F whose derivative is equal to f, i.e., F >' = f. The process of solving for antiderivatives is antidifferentiation (or indefinite integration.) Antiderivatives are related to definite integrals through the fundamental theorem of calculus: the definite integral of a function over an interval is equal to the difference between the values of an _____ evaluated at the endpoints of the interval.

   a. Integrand
   b. Antiderivative
   c. Indefinite integral
   d. Order of integration

2. In calculus, an antiderivative, primitive or _____ of a function f is a function F whose derivative is equal to f, i.e., F ' = f. The process of solving for antiderivatives is antidifferentiation (or indefinite integration.) Antiderivatives are related to definite integrals through the fundamental theorem of calculus: the definite integral of a function over an interval is equal to the difference between the values of an antiderivative evaluated at the endpoints of the interval.

   a. Arc length
   b. Integration by parts operator
   c. Indefinite integral
   d. Integral test for convergence

3. Integration is an important concept in mathematics, specifically in the field of calculus and, more broadly, mathematical analysis. Given a function f of a real variable x and an interval [a, b] of the real line, the _____

$$\int_a^b f(x)\,dx,$$

is defined informally to be the net signed area of the region in the xy-plane bounded by the graph of f, the x-axis, and the vertical lines x = a and x = b.

The term '_____' may also refer to the notion of antiderivative, a function F whose derivative is the given function f.

   a. Integral test for convergence
   b. Integrand
   c. Indefinite integral
   d. Integral

4. The _____ specifies the relationship between the two central operations of calculus, differentiation and integration.

The first part of the theorem, sometimes called the first _____, shows that an indefinite integration can be reversed by a differentiation.

The second part, sometimes called the second _____, allows one to compute the definite integral of a function by using any one of its infinitely many antiderivatives.

   a. Periodic function
   b. Leibniz formula
   c. Limits of integration
   d. Fundamental Theorem of Calculus

Chapter 6. CONSTRUCTING ANTIDERIVATIVES

5. In mathematics, a _____ (or critical number) is a point on the domain of a function where:

   - one dimension: the derivative (or slope of the line when visualized) is equal to zero or a point where the function ceases to be differentiable.
   - in general: there are two distinct concepts: either the derivative (Jacobian) vanishes, or it is not of full rank (or, in either case, the function is not differentiable); these agree in one dimension.

Note that in one dimension, a critical value or critical number x of function f is the domain element at which the derivative is zero or undefined, whereas the associated ordered pair (x, y) is the _____. In higher dimensions a critical value is in the range whereas a _____ is in the domain.

There are two situations in which a point becomes a _____ of a function of one variable. The first of which is that the value of the first derivative is equal to zero.

   a. Total derivative
   b. Multivariable calculus
   c. Differentiation operator
   d. Critical point

6. In differential calculus, an inflection point, or _____ (or inflexion) is a point on a curve at which the curvature changes sign. The curve changes from being concave upwards (positive curvature) to concave downwards (negative curvature), or vice versa. If one imagines driving a vehicle along the curve, it is a point at which the steering-wheel is momentarily 'straight', being turned from left to right or vice versa.
   a. Logarithmic derivative
   b. Lin-Tsien equation
   c. Derivative of a constant
   d. Point of inflection

7. In physics, and more specifically kinematics, _____ is the change in velocity over time. Because velocity is a vector, it can change in two ways: a change in magnitude and/or a change in direction. In one dimension, _____ is the rate at which something speeds up or slows down.
   a. ALGOR
   b. AUSM
   c. Acceleration
   d. ACTRAN

8. In infinitesimal calculus, a _____ is traditionally an infinitesimally small change in a variable. For example, if x is a variable, then a change in the value of x is often denoted Δx (or δx when this change is considered to be small.) The _____ dx represents such a change, but is infinitely small.
   a. Local maximum
   b. The Method of Mechanical Theorems
   c. Differential
   d. Dirichlet integral

9. A _____ is a mathematical equation for an unknown function of one or several variables that relates the values of the function itself and of its derivatives of various orders. they play a prominent role in engineering, physics, economics and other disciplines.

A simplified real world example of a _____ is modeling the acceleration of a ball falling through the air (considering only gravity and air resistance.)

   a. Structural stability
   b. Phase line
   c. Caloric polynomial
   d. Differential equation

10. In mathematics, a _____ to an ordinary or partial differential equation is a function for which the derivatives appearing in the equation may not all exist but which is nonetheless deemed to satisfy the equation in some precisely defined sense. There are many different definitions of _____, appropriate for different classes of equations. One of the most important is based on the notion of distributions.

 a. Singular perturbation
 b. Structural stability
 c. Conserved quantity
 d. Weak solution

11. In mathematics, in the field of differential equations, an initial value problem is an ordinary differential equation together with specified value, called the _____, of the unknown function at a given point in the domain of the solution. In physics or other sciences, modeling a system frequently amounts to solving an initial value problem; in this context, the differential equation is an evolution equation specifying how, given initial conditions, the system will evolve with time.

An initial value problem is a differential equation

$$y'(t) = f(t, y(t)) \quad \text{with} \quad f : \mathbb{R} \times \mathbb{R} \to \mathbb{R}$$

together with a point in the domain of f

$$(t_0, y_0) \in \mathbb{R} \times \mathbb{R},$$

called the _____.

 a. ACTRAN
 b. ALGOR
 c. Initial condition
 d. AUSM

12. In mathematics, in the field of differential equations, an _____ is an ordinary differential equation together with specified value, called the initial condition, of the unknown function at a given point in the domain of the solution. In physics or other sciences, modeling a system frequently amounts to solving an _____; in this context, the differential equation is an evolution equation specifying how, given initial conditions, the system will evolve with time.

An _____ is a differential equation

$$y'(t) = f(t, y(t)) \quad \text{with} \quad f : \mathbb{R} \times \mathbb{R} \to \mathbb{R}$$

together with a point in the domain of f

$$(t_0, y_0) \in \mathbb{R} \times \mathbb{R},$$

called the initial condition.

 a. ACTRAN
 b. AUSM
 c. Initial value problem
 d. ALGOR

Chapter 6. CONSTRUCTING ANTIDERIVATIVES

13. In mathematics, the _____ of a function y = f(x) is a function that, in some fashion, 'undoes' the effect of f The _____ of f is denoted f^{-1}. The statements y=f(x) and x=f^{-1}(y) are equivalent.
    a. ALGOR
    b. ACTRAN
    c. AUSM
    d. Inverse

Chapter 7. INTEGRATION

1. In a totally ordered set all elements are mutually comparable, so such a set can have at most one minimal element and at most one maximal element. Then, due to mutual comparability, the minimal element will also be the least element and the maximal element will also be the greatest element. Thus in a totally ordered set we can simply use the terms minimum and _____.

   a. Maximum
   b. Nth term
   c. Racetrack principle
   d. Leibniz rule

2. In calculus, the _____ is a formula for the derivative of the composite of two functions.

   In intuitive terms, if a variable, y, depends on a second variable, u, which in turn depends on a third variable, x, then the rate of change of y with respect to x can be computed as the rate of change of y with respect to u multiplied by the rate of change of u with respect to x. Schematically,

   $$\frac{dy}{dx} = \frac{dy}{du} \cdot \frac{du}{dx}.$$

   a. Chain rule
   b. Product rule
   c. Differentiation rules
   d. Reciprocal Rule

3. In economics, the _____ functional form of production functions is widely used to represent the relationship of an output to inputs. It was proposed by Knut Wicksell (1851-1926), and tested against statistical evidence by Charles Cobb and Paul Douglas in 1900-1928.

   For production, the function is

   $Y = AL^\alpha K^\beta$,

   where:

   - Y = total production (the monetary value of all goods produced in a year)
   - L = labor input
   - K = capital input
   - A = total factor productivity
   - α and β are the output elasticities of labor and capital, respectively. These values are constants determined by available technology.

   Output elasticity measures the responsiveness of output to a change in levels of either labor or capital used in production, ceteris paribus. For example if α = 0.15, a 1% increase in labor would lead to approximately a 0.15% increase in output.

   a. BDDC
   b. BIBO stability
   c. 15 theorem
   d. Cobb-Douglas

4. In mathematics, an _____ is a function built from a finite number of exponentials, logarithms, constants, one variable, and nth roots through composition and combinations using the four elementary operations (+ - × ÷.) The trigonometric functions and their inverses are assumed to be included in the elementary functions by using complex variables and the relations between the trigonometric functions and the exponential and logarithm functions.

Elementary functions are considered a subset of special functions.

a. ALGOR
b. AUSM
c. ACTRAN
d. Elementary function

5. In integral calculus we would want to write a fractional algebraic expression as the sum of its _____ in order to take the integral of each simple fraction separately. Once the original denominator, D_0, has been factored we set up a fraction for each factor in the denominator. We may use a subscripted D to represent the denominator of the respective _____ which are the factors in D_0.

a. Left inverse
b. Multinomial theorem
c. Closed-form expression
d. Partial fractions

6. Integration is an important concept in mathematics, specifically in the field of calculus and, more broadly, mathematical analysis. Given a function f of a real variable x and an interval [a, b] of the real line, the _____

$$\int_a^b f(x)\,dx,$$

is defined informally to be the net signed area of the region in the xy-plane bounded by the graph of f, the x-axis, and the vertical lines x = a and x = b.

The term '_____' may also refer to the notion of antiderivative, a function F whose derivative is the given function f.

a. Integrand
b. Integral
c. Indefinite integral
d. Integral test for convergence

7. In calculus, an antiderivative, primitive or _____ of a function f is a function F whose derivative is equal to f, i.e., F ' = f. The process of solving for antiderivatives is antidifferentiation (or indefinite integration.) Antiderivatives are related to definite integrals through the fundamental theorem of calculus: the definite integral of a function over an interval is equal to the difference between the values of an antiderivative evaluated at the endpoints of the interval.

a. Integration by parts operator
b. Arc length
c. Integral test for convergence
d. Indefinite integral

8. In mathematics, the concept of a '_____' is used to describe the behavior of a function as its argument or input either 'gets close' to some point, or as the argument becomes arbitrarily large; or the behavior of a sequence's elements as their index increases indefinitely. Limits are used in calculus and other branches of mathematical analysis to define derivatives and continuity.

In formulas, _____ is usually abbreviated as lim

a. BIBO stability b. 15 theorem
c. Limit d. BDDC

9. In calculus and mathematical analysis the _____ of the integral

$$\int_a^b f(x)\,dx$$

of a Riemann integrable function f defined on a closed and bounded interval [a, b] are the real numbers a and b.

_____ can also be defined for improper integrals, with the _____ of both

$$\lim_{z \to a+} \int_z^b f(x)\,dx$$

and

$$\lim_{z \to b-} \int_a^z f(x)\,dx$$

again being a and b. For an improper integral

$$\int_a^\infty f(x)\,dx$$

or

$$\int_{-\infty}^b f(x)\,dx$$

the _____ are a and ∞, or −∞ and b, respectively.

a. Differential b. Limits of integration
c. Maxima d. Test for Divergence

10. In mathematics, _____ are equalities that involve trigonometric functions that are true for every single value of the occurring variables. These identities are useful whenever expressions involving trigonometric functions need to be simplified. An important application is the integration of non-trigonometric functions: a common technique involves first using the substitution rule with a trigonometric function, and then simplifying the resulting integral with a trigonometric identity.
a. BDDC b. 15 theorem
c. BIBO stability d. Trigonometric identities

Chapter 7. INTEGRATION

11. Trigonometry is a branch of mathematics that deals with triangles, particularly those plane triangles in which one angle has 90 degrees (right triangles.) Trigonometry deals with relationships between the sides and the angles of triangles and with the _____ functions, which describe those relationships.

Trigonometry has applications in both pure mathematics and in applied mathematics, where it is essential in many branches of science and technology.

- a. Trigonometric
- b. Trigonometric integrals
- c. Sine
- d. Trigonometric functions

12. In mathematics, trigonometric identities are equalities that involve trigonometric functions that are true for every single value of the occurring variables. These identities are useful whenever expressions involving trigonometric functions need to be simplified. An important application is the integration of non-trigonometric functions: a common technique involves first using the substitution rule with a trigonometric function, and then simplifying the resulting integral with a _____.
- a. BDDC
- b. 15 theorem
- c. BIBO stability
- d. Trigonometric identity

13. In mathematics, _____ refers to the rewriting of an expression into a simpler form. For example, the process of rewriting a fraction into one with the smallest whole-number denominator possible (while keeping the numerator an integer) is called 'reducing a fraction'. Rewriting a radical (or 'root') expression with the smallest possible whole number under the radical symbol is called 'reducing a radical'.
- a. Quartic
- b. Reduction
- c. BDDC
- d. 15 theorem

14. In elementary algebra, _____ is a technique for converting a quadratic polynomial of the form

$$ax^2 + bx + c$$

to the form

$$a(\cdots\cdots)^2 + \text{constant}.$$

The expression inside the parenthesis is of the form x − constant. Thus one converts ax² + bx + c to

$$a(x - h)^2 + k$$

and one must find h and k.

Chapter 7. INTEGRATION

_____ is used in

- solving quadratic equations,
- graphing quadratic functions,
- evaluating integrals in calculus,
- finding Laplace transforms.

In mathematics, _____ is considered a basic algebraic operation, and is often applied without remark in any computation involving quadratic polynomials.

There is a simple formula in elementary algebra for computing the square of a binomial:

$$(x+p)^2 = x^2 + 2px + p^2.$$

For example:

$$(x+3)^2 = x^2 + 6x + 9 \qquad (p=3)$$
$$(x-5)^2 = x^2 - 10x + 25 \qquad (p=-5).$$

In any perfect square, the number p is always half the coefficient of x, and then the constant term is equal to p^2.

a. Hurwitz quaternion order
c. Multinomial theorem

b. Closed-form expression
d. Completing the square

15. In mathematics, the _____ is a statistical measure of the magnitude of a varying quantity. It is especially useful when variates are positive and negative, e.g., sinusoids.

It can be calculated for a series of discrete values or for a continuously varying function.

a. BIBO stability
c. BDDC

b. Root mean square
d. 15 theorem

16. In probability theory and statistics, the _____ (or expectation value or mean and for continuous random variables with a density function it is the probability density -weighted integral of the possible values.

The term '_____' can be misleading.

a. ACTRAN
c. ALGOR

b. AUSM
d. Expected value

17. In mathematics, _____ is the substitution of trigonometric functions for other expressions. One may use the trigonometric identities to simplify certain integrals containing radical expressions:

- If the integrand contains
$$\sqrt{a^2 - x^2},$$
let
$$x = a\sin\theta$$
and use the identity
$$1 - \sin^2\theta = \cos^2\theta.$$

- If the integrand contains
$$\sqrt{a^2 + x^2}$$
let $x = a\tan\theta$
and use the identity
$$1 + \tan^2\theta = \sec^2\theta.$$

- If the integrand contains
$$\sqrt{x^2 - a^2}$$
let
$$x = a\sec\theta$$
and use the identity
$$\sec^2\theta - 1 = \tan^2\theta.$$

In the integral
$$\int \frac{dx}{\sqrt{a^2 - x^2}}$$

we may use

$$x = a\sin(\theta), \; dx = a\cos(\theta)\, d\theta$$
$$\theta = \arcsin\left(\frac{x}{a}\right)$$

so that the integral becomes

$$\int \frac{dx}{\sqrt{a^2 - x^2}} = \int \frac{a\cos(\theta)\, d\theta}{\sqrt{a^2 - a^2\sin^2(\theta)}} = \int \frac{a\cos(\theta)\, d\theta}{\sqrt{a^2(1 - \sin^2(\theta))}}$$
$$= \int \frac{a\cos(\theta)\, d\theta}{\sqrt{a^2\cos^2(\theta)}} = \int d\theta = \theta + C = \arcsin\left(\frac{x}{a}\right) + C$$

Note that the above step requires that a > 0 and cos(θ) > 0; we can choose the a to be the positive square root of a^2; and we impose the restriction on θ to be −π/2 < θ < π/2 by using the arcsin function.

For a definite integral, one must figure out how the bounds of integration change. For example, as x goes from 0 to a/2, then sin (θ) goes from 0 to 1/2, so θ goes from 0 to π/6.

    a. Riemann sum   b. Surface of revolution
    c. Trigonometric substitution   d. Rectangle method

18. The _____ is a polynomial mapping of degree 2, often cited as an archetypal example of how complex, chaotic behaviour can arise from very simple non-linear dynamical equations. The map was popularized in a seminal 1976 paper by the biologist Robert May, in part as a discrete-time demographic model analogous to the logistic equation first created by Pierre François Verhulst. Mathematically, the _____ is written

$$(1) \quad x_{n+1} = r x_n (1 - x_n)$$

where:

        x_n is a number between zero and one, and represents the population at year n, and hence x_0 represents the initial population (at year 0)

        r is a positive number, and represents a combined rate for reproduction and starvation.

    a. Logistic map   b. BIBO stability
    c. 15 theorem   d. BDDC

19. In mathematics, a _____ is a method for approximating the total area underneath a curve on a graph, otherwise known as an integral. It may also be used to define the integration operation.

Chapter 7. INTEGRATION

Consider a function $f: D \rightarrow \mathbf{R}$, where D is a subset of the real numbers $\mathbf{R}$, and let $I = [a, b]$ be a closed interval contained in D. A finite set of points $\{x_0, x_1, x_2, \ldots x_n\}$ such that $a = x_0 < x_1 < x_2 \ldots < x_n = b$ creates a partition

$$P = \{[x_0, x_1), [x_1, x_2), \ldots [x_{n-1}, x_n]\}$$

of I.

a. Riemann sum
b. Solid of revolution
c. Risch algorithm
d. Signed measure

20. In mathematics, a _____ is a function which preserves the given order. This concept first arose in calculus, and was later generalized to the more abstract setting of order theory.

In calculus, a function f defined on a subset of the real numbers with real values is called monotonic (also monotonically increasing or non-decreasing), if for all x and y such that x >≤ y one has f(x) >≤ f(y), so f preserves the order.

a. 15 theorem
b. Pseudo-differential operator
c. Pettis integral
d. Monotonic function

21. In mathematics and its applications, a _____ system is a system for assigning an n-tuple of numbers or scalars to each point in an n-dimensional space. This concept is part of the theory of manifolds. 'Scalars' in many cases means real numbers, but, depending on context, can mean complex numbers or elements of some other commutative ring.

a. Cylindrical coordinate system
b. Spherical coordinate system
c. Coordinate
d. 15 theorem

22. In numerical analysis, _____ constitutes a broad family of algorithms for calculating the numerical value of a definite integral, and by extension, the term is also sometimes used to describe the numerical solution of differential equations The term numerical quadrature is more or less a synonym for _____, especially as applied to one-dimensional integrals.

a. Galerkin methods
b. Multigrid method
c. Meshfree methods
d. Numerical integration

23. In calculus, _____ gives a sequence of approximations of a differentiable function around a given point by polynomials (the Taylor polynomials of that function) whose coefficients depend only on the derivatives of the function at that point. The theorem also gives precise estimates on the size of the error in the approximation. The theorem is named after the mathematician Brook Taylor, who stated it in 1712, though the result was first discovered 41 years earlier in 1671 by James Gregory.

a. Taylor's theorem
b. Local minimum
c. Fresnel integrals
d. Related rates

24. If a function has an integral, it is said to be integrable. The function for which the integral is calculated is called the _____. The region over which a function is being integrated is called the domain of integration.

a. Order of integration
c. Integration by parts
b. Integral test for convergence
d. Integrand

25. In calculus, an _____ is the limit of a definite integral as an endpoint of the interval of integration approaches either a specified real number or ∞ or −∞ or, in some cases, as both endpoints approach limits.

Specifically, an _____ is a limit of the form

$$\lim_{b\to\infty} \int_a^b f(x)\,dx, \qquad \lim_{a\to-\infty} \int_a^b f(x)\,dx,$$

or of the form

$$\lim_{c\to b^-} \int_a^c f(x)\,dx, \qquad \lim_{c\to a^+} \int_c^b f(x)\,dx,$$

in which one takes a limit in one or the other (or sometimes both) endpoints . Improper integrals may also occur at an interior point of the domain of integration, or at multiple such points.

a. ALGOR
c. AUSM
b. ACTRAN
d. Improper integral

26. In acoustics and telecommunication, a _____ of a wave is a component frequency of the signal that is an integer multiple of the fundamental frequency. For example, if the fundamental frequency is f, the harmonics have frequencies f, 2f, 3f, 4f, etc. The harmonics have the property that they are all periodic at the fundamental frequency, therefore the sum of harmonics is also periodic at that frequency.

a. 15 theorem
c. Harmonic
b. BIBO stability
d. BDDC

27. In mathematics, the _____ is the infinite series

$$\sum_{k=1}^{\infty} \frac{1}{k} = 1 + \frac{1}{2} + \frac{1}{3} + \frac{1}{4} + \cdots.$$

Its name derives from the concept of overtones, or harmonics, in music: the wavelengths of the overtones of a vibrating string are 1/2, 1/3, 1/4, etc., of the string's fundamental wavelength. Every term of the series after the first is the harmonic mean of the neighboring terms; the term harmonic mean likewise derives from music.

The _____ diverges to infinity, albeit rather slowly (the first 10^{43} terms sum to less than 100 .)

a. 15 theorem
c. BIBO stability
b. BDDC
d. Harmonic series

Chapter 7. INTEGRATION

28. Cantor defined two kinds of _____ numbers, the ordinal numbers and the cardinal numbers. Ordinal numbers may be identified with well-ordered sets, or counting carried on to any stopping point, including points after an _____ number have already been counted. Generalizing finite and the ordinary _____ sequences which are maps from the positive integers leads to mappings from ordinal numbers, and transfinite sequences.

a. ALGOR
b. ACTRAN
c. Infinite
d. AUSM

29. In mathematics, a _____ decomposes a periodic function into a sum of simple oscillating functions, namely sines and cosines (or complex exponentials.) The study of _____ is a branch of Fourier analysis. _____ were introduced by Joseph Fourier (1768-1830) for the purpose of solving the heat equation in a metal plate.

a. 15 theorem
b. BDDC
c. BIBO stability
d. Fourier series

30. In mathematics, the _____ is an extension of the factorial function to real and complex numbers. For a complex number z with positive real part the _____ is defined by

$$\Gamma(z) = \int_0^\infty t^{z-1} e^{-t} \, dt \,.$$

This definition can be extended to the rest of the complex plane, excepting the non-positive integers.

If n is a positive integer, then

$$\Gamma(n) = (n-1)!,$$

showing the connection to the factorial function.

a. Digamma function
b. Gamma function
c. Multivariate gamma function
d. Pochhammer k-symbol

31. In mathematics, the _____, sometimes called the direct _____ is a criterion for convergence or divergence of a series whose terms are real or complex numbers. The test determines convergence by comparing the terms of the series in question with those of a series whose convergence properties are known.

The _____ states that if the series

$$\sum_{n=1}^\infty b_n$$

is an absolutely convergent series and

$$|a_n| \leq |b_n|$$

for sufficiently large n , then the series

$$\sum_{n=1}^{\infty} a_n$$

converges absolutely.

    a. Conditionally convergent   b. Ratio test
    c. Telescoping series   d. Comparison test

32. In mathematics, a _____ (or direction field) is a graphical representation of the solutions of a first-order differential equation. It is achieved without solving the differential equation analytically, and thence it is useful. The representation may be used to qualitatively visualise solutions, or to numerically approximate them.
    a. Visual Calculus   b. Leibniz function
    c. Continuous function   d. Slope field

33. In geometry, the _____ (or simply the tangent) to a curve at a given point is the straight line that 'just touches' the curve at that point (in the sense explained more precisely below.) As it passes through the point of tangency, the _____ is 'going in the same direction' as the curve, and in this sense it is the best straight-line approximation to the curve at that point. The same definition applies to space curves and curves in n-dimensional Euclidean space.
    a. Lie derivative   b. Minimal surface
    c. North pole   d. Tangent line

Chapter 8. USING THE DEFINITE INTEGRAL

1. The _____ specifies the relationship between the two central operations of calculus, differentiation and integration.

The first part of the theorem, sometimes called the first _____, shows that an indefinite integration can be reversed by a differentiation.

The second part, sometimes called the second _____, allows one to compute the definite integral of a function by using any one of its infinitely many antiderivatives.

a. Periodic function
c. Leibniz formula
b. Limits of integration
d. Fundamental Theorem of Calculus

2. In mathematics, a _____ is a method for approximating the total area underneath a curve on a graph, otherwise known as an integral. It may also be used to define the integration operation.

Consider a function $f: D \rightarrowtail R$, where D is a subset of the real numbers R, and let $I = [a, b]$ be a closed interval contained in D. A finite set of points $\{x_0, x_1, x_2, ... x_n\}$ such that $a = x_0 < x_1 < x_2 ... < x_n = b$ creates a partition

$$P = \{[x_0, x_1), [x_1, x_2), ... [x_{n-1}, x_n]\}$$

of I.

a. Riemann sum
c. Risch algorithm
b. Solid of revolution
d. Signed measure

3. In mathematics, engineering, and manufacturing, a _____ is a solid figure obtained by rotating a plane curve around some straight line (the axis) that lies on the same plane.

Assuming that the curve does not cross the axis, the solid's volume is equal to the length of the circle described by the figure's centroid, times the figure's area (Pappus's second centroid Theorem.)

Rotating a curve

A representative disk is a three-dimensional volume element of a _____.

a. Surface of revolution
c. Trigonometric substitution
b. Solid of revolution
d. Riemann sum

4. For some curves there is a smallest number L that is an upper bound on the length of any polygonal approximation. If such a number exists, then the curve is said to be rectifiable and the curve is defined to have _____ L.

Let C be a curve in Euclidean (or, generally, a metric) space $X = R^n$, so C is the image of a continuous function $f : [a, b] \rightarrow X$ of the interval [a, b] into X.

a. Arc length
c. Integrand
b. Order of integration
d. Integration by parametric derivatives

5. Integration is an important concept in mathematics, specifically in the field of calculus and, more broadly, mathematical analysis. Given a function f of a real variable x and an interval [a, b] of the real line, the _____

$$\int_a^b f(x)\, dx,$$

is defined informally to be the net signed area of the region in the xy-plane bounded by the graph of f, the x-axis, and the vertical lines x = a and x = b.

The term '_____' may also refer to the notion of antiderivative, a function F whose derivative is the given function f.

a. Integral test for convergence
c. Integrand
b. Indefinite integral
d. Integral

6. _____ is the long dimension of any object. The _____ of a thing is the distance between its ends, its linear extent as measured from end to end. This may be distinguished from height, which is vertical extent, and width or breadth, which are the distance from side to side, measuring across the object at right angles to the _____.

a. Length
c. 15 theorem
b. BDDC
d. BIBO stability

7. In mathematics, a (topological) _____ is defined as follows: let I be an interval of real numbers (i.e. a non-empty connected subset of $\mathbb{R}$); then a _____ γ is a continuous mapping $\gamma : I \to X$, where X is a topological space. The _____ γ is said to be simple if it is injective, i.e. if for all x, y in I, we have $\gamma(x) = \gamma(y) \implies x = y$. If I is a closed bounded interval $[a, b]$, we also allow the possibility $\gamma(a) = \gamma(b)$ (this convention makes it possible to talk about closed simple _____.)

a. Tractrix
c. Curve
b. Prolate cycloid
d. Closed curve

8. Determining the _____ segment -- also called rectification of a curve -- was historically difficult. Although many methods were used for specific curves, the advent of calculus led to a general formula that provides closed-form solutions in some cases.

A curve in, say, the plane can be approximated by connecting a finite number of points on the curve using line segments to create a polygonal path. Since it is straightforward to calculate the length of each linear segment (using the theorem of Pythagoras in Euclidean space, for example), the total length of the approximation can be found by summing the lengths of each linear segment.

a. Linearity of integration
c. Surface of revolution
b. Disk integration
d. Length of an irregular arc

Chapter 8. USING THE DEFINITE INTEGRAL

9. In physics and geometry, the _____ is the theoretical shape of a hanging flexible chain or cable when supported at its ends and acted upon by a uniform gravitational force (its own weight) and in equilibrium. The curve has a U shape that is similar in appearance to the parabola, though it is a different curve.

   a. 15 theorem
   b. Catenary
   c. BDDC
   d. BIBO stability

10. The _____ of a material is defined as its mass per unit volume. The symbol of _____ is ρ '>rho.)

Mathematically:

$$d = \frac{m}{V}$$

where:

    d is the _____,
    m is the mass,
    V is the volume.

   a. Density
   b. BIBO stability
   c. 15 theorem
   d. BDDC

11. The concept of _____ in mathematics evolved from the concept of _____ in physics. The nth _____ of a real-valued function f(x) of a real variable about a value c is

$$\mu'_n = \int_{-\infty}^{\infty} (x - c)^n f(x)\, dx.$$

It is possible to define moments for random variables in a more general fashion than moments for real values. See Moments in metric spaces.

   a. Poisson distribution
   b. Moment
   c. Geometric mean
   d. Median

12. In elementary algebra, _____ is a technique for converting a quadratic polynomial of the form

$$ax^2 + bx + c$$

to the form

$$a(\cdots\cdots)^2 + \text{constant}.$$

Chapter 8. USING THE DEFINITE INTEGRAL

The expression inside the parenthesis is of the form x − constant. Thus one converts ax² + bx + c to

$$a(x-h)^2 + k$$

and one must find h and k.

_____ is used in

- solving quadratic equations,
- graphing quadratic functions,
- evaluating integrals in calculus,
- finding Laplace transforms.

In mathematics, _____ is considered a basic algebraic operation, and is often applied without remark in any computation involving quadratic polynomials.

There is a simple formula in elementary algebra for computing the square of a binomial:

$$(x+p)^2 = x^2 + 2px + p^2.$$

For example:

$$(x+3)^2 = x^2 + 6x + 9 \qquad (p=3)$$
$$(x-5)^2 = x^2 - 10x + 25 \qquad (p=-5).$$

In any perfect square, the number p is always half the coefficient of x, and then the constant term is equal to p².

a. Hurwitz quaternion order
b. Completing the square
c. Multinomial theorem
d. Closed-form expression

13. If a function has an integral, it is said to be integrable. The function for which the integral is calculated is called the _____. The region over which a function is being integrated is called the domain of integration.
    a. Order of integration
    b. Integration by parts
    c. Integral test for convergence
    d. Integrand

14. In physics, and more specifically kinematics, _____ is the change in velocity over time. Because velocity is a vector, it can change in two ways: a change in magnitude and/or a change in direction. In one dimension, _____ is the rate at which something speeds up or slows down.
    a. AUSM
    b. ACTRAN
    c. Acceleration
    d. ALGOR

Chapter 8. USING THE DEFINITE INTEGRAL

15. _____ is the concept of adding accumulated interest back to the principal, so that interest is earned on interest from that moment on. The act of declaring interest to be principal is called compounding (i.e., interest is compounded.) A loan, for example, may have its interest compounded every month: in this case, a loan with $100 principal and 1% interest per month would have a balance of $101 at the end of the first month.

   a. BIBO stability
   b. 15 theorem
   c. Compound interest
   d. BDDC

16. In economics, the _____ functional form of production functions is widely used to represent the relationship of an output to inputs. It was proposed by Knut Wicksell (1851-1926), and tested against statistical evidence by Charles Cobb and Paul Douglas in 1900-1928.

For production, the function is

$$Y = AL^{\alpha}K^{\beta},$$

where:

- Y = total production (the monetary value of all goods produced in a year)
- L = labor input
- K = capital input
- A = total factor productivity
- α and β are the output elasticities of labor and capital, respectively. These values are constants determined by available technology.

Output elasticity measures the responsiveness of output to a change in levels of either labor or capital used in production, ceteris paribus. For example if α = 0.15, a 1% increase in labor would lead to approximately a 0.15% increase in output.

   a. BIBO stability
   b. BDDC
   c. Cobb-Douglas
   d. 15 theorem

17. In probability theory and statistics, the _____ or just distribution function, completely describes the probability distribution of a real-valued random variable X. For every real number x, the _____ of X is given by

$$x \mapsto F_X(x) = P(X \leq x),$$

where the right-hand side represents the probability that the random variable X takes on a value less than or equal to x. The probability that X lies in the interval (a, b] is therefore $F_X(b) - F_X(a)$ if a < b.

If treating several random variables X, Y, ...

   a. 15 theorem
   b. BDDC
   c. BIBO stability
   d. Cumulative distribution function

18. In probability theory and statistics, the _____ (or expectation value or mean and for continuous random variables with a density function it is the probability density -weighted integral of the possible values.

The term '_____' can be misleading.

a. ACTRAN
c. ALGOR
b. Expected value
d. AUSM

19. In probability theory and statistics, a _____ is described as the number separating the higher half of a sample, a population from the lower half. The _____ of a finite list of numbers can be found by arranging all the observations from lowest value to highest value and picking the middle one. If there is an even number of observations, the _____ is not unique, so one often takes the mean of the two middle values.

a. Median
c. Correlation
b. Moment
d. Geometric mean

20. The _____ is an important family of continuous probability distributions, applicable in many fields. Each member of the family may be defined by two parameters, location and scale: the mean and variance respectively. The standard _____ is the _____ with a mean of zero and a variance of one.

a. Moment
c. Continuous random variable
b. Correlation
d. Normal distribution

21. In statistics, _____ is a simple measure of the variability or dispersion of a data set. A low _____ indicates that all of the data points are very close to the same value (the mean), while high _____ indicates that the data is 'spread out' over a large range of values.

For example, the average height for adult men in the United States is about 70 inches, with a _____ of around 3 inches.

a. Correlation
c. Poisson distribution
b. Continuous random variable
d. Standard deviation

22. The _____ of an object is the extra energy which it possesses due to its motion. It is defined as the work needed to accelerate a body of a given mass from rest to its current velocity. Having gained this energy during its acceleration, the body maintains this _____ unless its speed changes.

a. 15 theorem
c. Law of Conservation of Energy
b. Kinetic energy
d. BDDC

23. _____ is how much exposed area an object has. It is expressed in square units. If an object has flat faces, its _____ can be calculated by adding together the areas of its faces.

a. Surface area
c. Vector area
b. Lipschitz domain
d. Plane curve

Chapter 9. SERIES

1. In mathematics, a _____ is a series with a constant ratio between successive terms. For example, the series

$$\frac{1}{2} + \frac{1}{4} + \frac{1}{8} + \frac{1}{16} + \cdots$$

is geometric, because each term is equal to half of the previous term. The sum of this series is 1, as illustrated in the following picture:

_____ are one of the simplest examples of infinite series with finite sums.

- a. Converge absolutely
- b. Conditionally convergent
- c. Sequence transformation
- d. Geometric series

2. Cantor defined two kinds of _____ numbers, the ordinal numbers and the cardinal numbers. Ordinal numbers may be identified with well-ordered sets, or counting carried on to any stopping point, including points after an _____ number have already been counted. Generalizing finite and the ordinary _____ sequences which are maps from the positive integers leads to mappings from ordinal numbers, and transfinite sequences.
- a. ALGOR
- b. AUSM
- c. ACTRAN
- d. Infinite

3. The terms of the series are often produced according to a certain rule, such as by a formula, by an algorithm, by a sequence of measurements, or even by a random number generator. As there are an infinite number of terms, this notion is often called an _____. Unlike finite summations, series need tools from mathematical analysis to be fully understood and manipulated.
- a. Extreme value
- b. Integration by substitution
- c. Extreme Value Theorem
- d. Infinite series

4. A _____ is an expression which compares quantities relative to each other. The most common examples involve two quantities, but in theory any number of quantities can be compared. In mathematical terms, they are represented by separating each quantity with a colon, for example the _____ 2:3, which is read as the _____ 'two to three'.
- a. 15 theorem
- b. Sequence
- c. Ratio
- d. Y-intercept

5. Call S_N the _____ to N of the sequence $\{a_n\}$, or _____ of the series. A series is the sequence of partial sums, $\{S_N\}$.

When talking about series, one can refer either to the sequence $\{S_N\}$ of the partial sums, or to the sum of the series,

$$\sum_{n=0}^{\infty} a_n$$

i.e., the limit of the sequence of partial sums - it is clear which one is meant from context.

a. The Method of Mechanical Theorems
b. Dirichlet integral
c. Maxima
d. Partial sum

6. In mathematics and its applications, a _____ system is a system for assigning an n-tuple of numbers or scalars to each point in an n-dimensional space. This concept is part of the theory of manifolds. 'Scalars' in many cases means real numbers, but, depending on context, can mean complex numbers or elements of some other commutative ring.
a. Spherical coordinate system
b. Cylindrical coordinate system
c. 15 theorem
d. Coordinate

7. In vector calculus, the _____ is an operator that measures the magnitude of a vector field's source or sink at a given point; the _____ of a vector field is a (signed) scalar. For example, consider air as it is heated or cooled. The relevant vector field for this example is the velocity of the moving air at a point.
a. Triple product
b. Green's theorem
c. Gradient theorem
d. Divergence

8. In acoustics and telecommunication, a _____ of a wave is a component frequency of the signal that is an integer multiple of the fundamental frequency. For example, if the fundamental frequency is f, the harmonics have frequencies f, 2f, 3f, 4f, etc. The harmonics have the property that they are all periodic at the fundamental frequency, therefore the sum of harmonics is also periodic at that frequency.
a. BDDC
b. BIBO stability
c. Harmonic
d. 15 theorem

9. In mathematics, the _____ is the infinite series

$$\sum_{k=1}^{\infty} \frac{1}{k} = 1 + \frac{1}{2} + \frac{1}{3} + \frac{1}{4} + \cdots.$$

Its name derives from the concept of overtones, or harmonics, in music: the wavelengths of the overtones of a vibrating string are 1/2, 1/3, 1/4, etc., of the string's fundamental wavelength. Every term of the series after the first is the harmonic mean of the neighboring terms; the term harmonic mean likewise derives from music.

The _____ diverges to infinity, albeit rather slowly (the first 10^{43} terms sum to less than 100 .)

a. 15 theorem
b. BDDC
c. BIBO stability
d. Harmonic series

10. In mathematics, a _____ is an ordered list of objects (or events). Like a set, it contains members (also called elements or terms), and the number of terms (possibly infinite) is called the length of the _____. Unlike a set, order matters, and the exact same elements can appear multiple times at different positions in the _____.
a. 15 theorem
b. Sequence
c. Y-intercept
d. Slope

11. Integration is an important concept in mathematics, specifically in the field of calculus and, more broadly, mathematical analysis. Given a function f of a real variable x and an interval [a, b] of the real line, the _____

$$\int_a^b f(x)\,dx,$$

is defined informally to be the net signed area of the region in the xy-plane bounded by the graph of f, the x-axis, and the vertical lines x = a and x = b.

The term '_____' may also refer to the notion of antiderivative, a function F whose derivative is the given function f.

a. Indefinite integral
c. Integral test for convergence
b. Integral
d. Integrand

12. In mathematics, the _____ for convergence is a method used to test infinite series of non-negative terms for convergence. An early form of the test of convergence was developed in India by Madhava in the 14th century, and by his followers at the Kerala School. In Europe, it was later developed by Maclaurin and Cauchy and is sometimes known as the Maclaurin-Cauchy test.

a. Integral test
c. AUSM
b. ACTRAN
d. ALGOR

13. In mathematics, the _____, sometimes called the direct _____ is a criterion for convergence or divergence of a series whose terms are real or complex numbers. The test determines convergence by comparing the terms of the series in question with those of a series whose convergence properties are known.

The _____ states that if the series

$$\sum_{n=1}^{\infty} b_n$$

is an absolutely convergent series and

$$|a_n| \leq |b_n|$$

for sufficiently large n , then the series

$$\sum_{n=1}^{\infty} a_n$$

converges absolutely.

a. Ratio test
c. Conditionally convergent
b. Telescoping series
d. Comparison test

Chapter 9. SERIES

14. In calculus, an _____ is the limit of a definite integral as an endpoint of the interval of integration approaches either a specified real number or ∞ or −∞ or, in some cases, as both endpoints approach limits.

Specifically, an _____ is a limit of the form

$$\lim_{b\to\infty} \int_a^b f(x)\,dx, \qquad \lim_{a\to-\infty} \int_a^b f(x)\,dx,$$

or of the form

$$\lim_{c\to b^-} \int_a^c f(x)\,dx, \qquad \lim_{c\to a^+} \int_c^b f(x)\,dx,$$

in which one takes a limit in one or the other (or sometimes both) endpoints . Improper integrals may also occur at an interior point of the domain of integration, or at multiple such points.

 a. ACTRAN
 b. AUSM
 c. ALGOR
 d. Improper integral

15. In mathematics, the _____ is a test (or 'criterion') for the convergence of a series

$$\sum_{n=0}^{\infty} a_n$$

whose terms are real or complex numbers. The test was first published by Jean le Rond d'Alembert and is sometimes known as d'Alembert's _____. The test makes use of the number

()

in the cases where this limit exists.

 a. Geometric series
 b. Converge absolutely
 c. Telescoping series
 d. Ratio test

16. In mathematics, the _____ of a power series is a non-negative quantity, either a real number or ∞, that represents a domain (within the radius) in which the series will converge. Within the _____, a power series converges absolutely and uniformly on compacta as well. If the series converges, it is the Taylor series of the analytic function to which it converges inside its _____.

 a. Blaschke product
 b. Holomorphically separable
 c. Branch point
 d. Radius of convergence

17. In mathematics, an _____ is an infinite series of the form

$$\sum_{n=0}^{\infty}(-1)^n a_n,$$

with $a_n \geq 0$ (or $a_n \leq 0$) for all n. A finite sum of this kind is an alternating sum. An _____ converges if the terms a_n converge to 0 monotonically.

a. Alternating series
c. Infinite series

b. Uniform convergence
d. Extreme value

18. In mathematics, a _____ (in one variable) is an infinite series of the form

$$f(x) = \sum_{n=0}^{\infty} a_n (x-c)^n = a_0 + a_1(x-c)^1 + a_2(x-c)^2 + a_3(x-c)^3 + \cdots$$

where a_n represents the coefficient of the nth term, c is a constant, and x varies around c (for this reason one sometimes speaks of the series as being centered at c

In many situations c is equal to zero, for instance when considering a Maclaurin series.

a. Differential coefficient
c. Power series

b. Stationary phase approximation
d. Differential calculus

Chapter 10. APPROXIMATING FUNCTIONS

1. In mathematics, a _____ is an approximation of a general function using a linear function (more precisely, an affine function.)

Given a differentiable function f of one real variable, Taylor's theorem for n=1 states that

$$f(x) = f(a) + f'(a)(x-a) + R_2$$

where R_2 is the remainder term. The _____ is obtained by dropping the remainder:

$$f(x) \approx f(a) + f'(a)(x-a)$$

which is true for x close to a.

a. Lin-Tsien equation
b. Point of inflection
c. Smooth function
d. Linear approximation

2. In geometry, the _____ (or simply the tangent) to a curve at a given point is the straight line that 'just touches' the curve at that point (in the sense explained more precisely below.) As it passes through the point of tangency, the _____ is 'going in the same direction' as the curve, and in this sense it is the best straight-line approximation to the curve at that point. The same definition applies to space curves and curves in n-dimensional Euclidean space.

a. Tangent line
b. Lie derivative
c. North pole
d. Minimal surface

3. In calculus, _____ gives a sequence of approximations of a differentiable function around a given point by polynomials (the Taylor polynomials of that function) whose coefficients depend only on the derivatives of the function at that point. The theorem also gives precise estimates on the size of the error in the approximation. The theorem is named after the mathematician Brook Taylor, who stated it in 1712, though the result was first discovered 41 years earlier in 1671 by James Gregory.

a. Related rates
b. Fresnel integrals
c. Local minimum
d. Taylor's theorem

4. In mathematics, the _____ of a non-negative integer n, denoted by n!, is the product of all positive integers less than or equal to n. For example,

$$5! = 1 \times 2 \times 3 \times 4 \times 5 = 120$$

and

$$6! = 1 \times 2 \times 3 \times 4 \times 5 \times 6 = 720.$$

The notation n! was introduced by Christian Kramp in 1808.

Chapter 10. APPROXIMATING FUNCTIONS

The _____ function is formally defined by

$$n! = \prod_{k=1}^{n} k \qquad \forall n \in \mathbb{N}$$

or recursively defined by

$$n! = \begin{cases} n \leq 1 & 1 \\ n > 1 & n(n-1)! \end{cases} \qquad \forall n \in \mathbb{N}.$$

Both of the above definitions incorporate the instance

$$0! = 1$$

as an instance of the fact that the product of no numbers at all is 1.

a. Factorial
c. BDDC
b. Constraint counting
d. 15 theorem

5. The _____ of an angle is the ratio of the length of the opposite side to the length of the hypotenuse. In our case

$$\sin A = \frac{\text{opposite}}{\text{hypotenuse}} = \frac{a}{h}.$$

Note that this ratio does not depend on size of the particular right triangle chosen, as long as it contains the angle A, since all such triangles are similar.

The cosine of an angle is the ratio of the length of the adjacent side to the length of the hypotenuse.

a. Trigonometric
c. Trigonometric functions
b. Sine integral
d. Sine

6. In mathematics, the _____ is a representation of a function as an infinite sum of terms calculated from the values of its derivatives at a single point. It may be regarded as the limit of the Taylor polynomials. If the series is centered at zero, the series is also called a Maclaurin series.

a. 15 theorem
c. BIBO stability
b. BDDC
d. Taylor series

7. In mathematics, a _____ (in one variable) is an infinite series of the form

Chapter 10. APPROXIMATING FUNCTIONS

$$f(x) = \sum_{n=0}^{\infty} a_n (x-c)^n = a_0 + a_1(x-c)^1 + a_2(x-c)^2 + a_3(x-c)^3 + \cdots$$

where a_n represents the coefficient of the nth term, c is a constant, and x varies around c (for this reason one sometimes speaks of the series as being centered at c

In many situations c is equal to zero, for instance when considering a Maclaurin series.

a. Differential calculus
b. Differential coefficient
c. Power series
d. Stationary phase approximation

8. In mathematics, the _____ of a power series is a non-negative quantity, either a real number or ∞, that represents a domain (within the radius) in which the series will converge. Within the _____, a power series converges absolutely and uniformly on compacta as well. If the series converges, it is the Taylor series of the analytic function to which it converges inside its _____.

a. Radius of convergence
b. Holomorphically separable
c. Blaschke product
d. Branch point

9. In acoustics and telecommunication, a _____ of a wave is a component frequency of the signal that is an integer multiple of the fundamental frequency. For example, if the fundamental frequency is f, the harmonics have frequencies f, 2f, 3f, 4f, etc. The harmonics have the property that they are all periodic at the fundamental frequency, therefore the sum of harmonics is also periodic at that frequency.

a. 15 theorem
b. BDDC
c. BIBO stability
d. Harmonic

10. In mathematics, the _____ is the infinite series

$$\sum_{k=1}^{\infty} \frac{1}{k} = 1 + \frac{1}{2} + \frac{1}{3} + \frac{1}{4} + \cdots.$$

Its name derives from the concept of overtones, or harmonics, in music: the wavelengths of the overtones of a vibrating string are 1/2, 1/3, 1/4, etc., of the string's fundamental wavelength. Every term of the series after the first is the harmonic mean of the neighboring terms; the term harmonic mean likewise derives from music.

The _____ diverges to infinity, albeit rather slowly (the first 10^{43} terms sum to less than 100 .)

a. 15 theorem
b. BDDC
c. Harmonic series
d. BIBO stability

Chapter 10. APPROXIMATING FUNCTIONS

11. In elementary algebra, a _____ is a polynomial with two terms--the sum of two monomials--often bound by parenthesis or brackets when operated upon. It is the simplest kind of polynomial other than monomials.

- The _____ $a^2 - b^2$ can be factored as the product of two other binomials:

$$a^2 - b^2 = (a + b)(a - b.)$$

This is a special case of the more general formula:

$$a^{n+1} - b^{n+1} = (a-b) \sum_{k=0}^{n} a^k b^{n-k}.$$

- The product of a pair of linear binomials (ax + b) and (cx + d) is:

$$(ax + b)(cx + d) = acx^2 + axd + bcx + bd.$$

- A _____ raised to the nth power, represented as

$$(a + b)^n$$

can be expanded by means of the _____ theorem or, equivalently, using Pascal's triangle. Taking a simple example, the perfect square _____ $(p + q)^2$ can be found by squaring the :first digit, adding twice the product of the first and second digit and finally adding the square of the second digit, to give $p^2 + 2pq + q^2$.

a. Binomial
b. Completing the square
c. Multinomial theorem
d. Partial fractions

12. In mathematics, the _____ generalizes the purely algebraic formula of the binomial theorem to complex values of α. It is also a special case of a Newton series. The _____ is the series

$$(1+x)^\alpha = \sum_{k=0}^{\infty} \binom{\alpha}{k} x^k = \sum_{k=0}^{\infty} \frac{\prod_{a=0}^{k-1}(\alpha - a)\, x^k}{k!}$$

where α is a complex number and

$$\binom{\alpha}{k} = \frac{\alpha(\alpha - 1)(\alpha - 2) \cdots (\alpha - k + 1)}{k!}$$

is the (generalized) binomial coefficient (if α is a non negative integer, then the (α + 1) th term and all later terms in the series are zero, since each one contains a factor equal to (α - α): thus, in that case, the summation reduces to the algebraic binomial formula.)

a. Fresnel integrals
b. Maxima
c. Binomial series
d. Differential

13. In mathematics, a _____ is a series with a constant ratio between successive terms. For example, the series

Chapter 10. APPROXIMATING FUNCTIONS

$$\frac{1}{2} + \frac{1}{4} + \frac{1}{8} + \frac{1}{16} + \cdots$$

is geometric, because each term is equal to half of the previous term. The sum of this series is 1, as illustrated in the following picture:

_____ are one of the simplest examples of infinite series with finite sums.

a. Conditionally convergent
c. Sequence transformation
b. Converge absolutely
d. Geometric series

14. Integration is an important concept in mathematics, specifically in the field of calculus and, more broadly, mathematical analysis. Given a function f of a real variable x and an interval [a, b] of the real line, the _____

$$\int_a^b f(x)\, dx,$$

is defined informally to be the net signed area of the region in the xy-plane bounded by the graph of f, the x-axis, and the vertical lines x = a and x = b.

The term '_____' may also refer to the notion of antiderivative, a function F whose derivative is the given function f.

a. Integral test for convergence
c. Indefinite integral
b. Integrand
d. Integral

15. In calculus, a branch of mathematics, the _____ is a measurement of how a function changes when its input changes. Loosely speaking, a _____ can be thought of as how much a quantity is changing at some given point. For example, the _____ of the position (or distance) of a vehicle with respect to time is the instantaneous velocity (respectively, instantaneous speed) at which the vehicle is traveling.

The process of finding a _____ is called differentiation. The fundamental theorem of calculus states that differentiation is the reverse process to integration.

a. Stationary phase approximation
c. Bounded function
b. Semi-differentiability
d. Derivative

16. In physics, and more specifically kinematics, _____ is the change in velocity over time. Because velocity is a vector, it can change in two ways: a change in magnitude and/or a change in direction. In one dimension, _____ is the rate at which something speeds up or slows down.

a. Acceleration
c. ACTRAN
b. ALGOR
d. AUSM

Chapter 10. APPROXIMATING FUNCTIONS

17. The _____ in some data is the discrepancy between an exact value and some approximation to it. An _____ can occur because

   1. the measurement of the data is not precise (due to the instruments), or
   2. approximations are used instead of the real data (e.g., 3.14 instead of π.)

In the mathematical field of numerical analysis, the numerical stability of an algorithm in numerical analysis indicates how the error is propagated by the algorithm.

One commonly distinguishes between the relative error and the absolute error. The absolute error is the magnitude of the difference between the exact value and the approximation.

   a. ALGOR
   c. AUSM
   b. Approximation error
   d. ACTRAN

18. In mathematics, a _____ decomposes a periodic function into a sum of simple oscillating functions, namely sines and cosines (or complex exponentials.) The study of _____ is a branch of Fourier analysis. _____ were introduced by Joseph Fourier (1768-1830) for the purpose of solving the heat equation in a metal plate.
   a. BDDC
   c. BIBO stability
   b. Fourier series
   d. 15 theorem

19. In mathematics, a _____ is a constant multiplicative factor of a certain object. For example, in the expression $9x^2$, the _____ of x^2 is 9.

The object can be such things as a variable, a vector, a function, etc.

   a. Resultant
   c. Degree of the polynomial
   b. Binomial type
   d. Coefficient

20. The _____, L, of a dynamical system is a function that summarizes the dynamics of the system. It is named after Joseph Louis Lagrange. The concept of a _____ was originally introduced in a reformulation of classical mechanics known as _____ mechanics.
   a. Klein-Gordon equation
   c. Lagrangian
   b. Vector potential
   d. Dirac equation

21. In economics, the _____ functional form of production functions is widely used to represent the relationship of an output to inputs. It was proposed by Knut Wicksell (1851-1926), and tested against statistical evidence by Charles Cobb and Paul Douglas in 1900-1928.

For production, the function is

$$Y = AL^{\alpha}K^{\beta},$$

where:

- Y = total production (the monetary value of all goods produced in a year)
- L = labor input
- K = capital input
- A = total factor productivity
- α and β are the output elasticities of labor and capital, respectively. These values are constants determined by available technology.

Output elasticity measures the responsiveness of output to a change in levels of either labor or capital used in production, ceteris paribus. For example if α = 0.15, a 1% increase in labor would lead to approximately a 0.15% increase in output.

a. Cobb-Douglas
c. 15 theorem
b. BIBO stability
d. BDDC

22. A _____ is a model used within physics to explain how gravity exists in the universe. In its original concept, gravity was a force between point masses. Following Newton, Laplace attempted to model gravity as some kind of radiation field or fluid, and since the 19th century explanations for gravity have usually been sought in terms of a field model, rather than a point attraction.

a. BIBO stability
c. Gravitational field
b. BDDC
d. 15 theorem

23. _____ can be thought of as energy stored within a physical system. It is called _____ because it has the potential to be converted into other forms of energy, such as kinetic energy, and to do work in the process. The standard (SI) unit of measure for _____ is the joule, the same as for work or energy in general.

a. 15 theorem
c. BDDC
b. Law of Conservation of Energy
d. Potential energy

24. A _____ is a mathematical expression of the form f(x + b) − f(x + a.) If a _____ is divided by b − a, one gets a difference quotient. The approximation of derivatives by finite differences plays a central role in _____ methods for the numerical solution of differential equations, especially boundary value problems.

a. Discrete Poisson equation
c. Finite difference
b. Geodesic grid
d. Finite-difference methods

Chapter 11. DIFFERENTIAL EQUATIONS

1. In infinitesimal calculus, a _____ is traditionally an infinitesimally small change in a variable. For example, if x is a variable, then a change in the value of x is often denoted Δx (or δx when this change is considered to be small.) The _____ dx represents such a change, but is infinitely small.

   a. Differential
   b. Local maximum
   c. Dirichlet integral
   d. The Method of Mechanical Theorems

2. A _____ is a mathematical equation for an unknown function of one or several variables that relates the values of the function itself and of its derivatives of various orders. they play a prominent role in engineering, physics, economics and other disciplines.

   A simplified real world example of a _____ is modeling the acceleration of a ball falling through the air (considering only gravity and air resistance.)

   a. Phase line
   b. Caloric polynomial
   c. Structural stability
   d. Differential equation

3. In mathematics, in the field of differential equations, an _____ is an ordinary differential equation together with specified value, called the initial condition, of the unknown function at a given point in the domain of the solution. In physics or other sciences, modeling a system frequently amounts to solving an _____; in this context, the differential equation is an evolution equation specifying how, given initial conditions, the system will evolve with time.

   An _____ is a differential equation

   $$y'(t) = f(t, y(t)) \quad \text{with} \quad f : \mathbb{R} \times \mathbb{R} \to \mathbb{R}$$

   together with a point in the domain of f

   $$(t_0, y_0) \in \mathbb{R} \times \mathbb{R},$$

   called the initial condition.

   a. AUSM
   b. Initial value problem
   c. ACTRAN
   d. ALGOR

4. In mathematics, a _____ to an ordinary or partial differential equation is a function for which the derivatives appearing in the equation may not all exist but which is nonetheless deemed to satisfy the equation in some precisely defined sense. There are many different definitions of _____, appropriate for different classes of equations. One of the most important is based on the notion of distributions.

   a. Singular perturbation
   b. Structural stability
   c. Weak solution
   d. Conserved quantity

5. In mathematics, in the field of differential equations, an initial value problem is an ordinary differential equation together with specified value, called the _____, of the unknown function at a given point in the domain of the solution. In physics or other sciences, modeling a system frequently amounts to solving an initial value problem; in this context, the differential equation is an evolution equation specifying how, given initial conditions, the system will evolve with time.

An initial value problem is a differential equation

$$y'(t) = f(t, y(t)) \quad \text{with} \quad f : \mathbb{R} \times \mathbb{R} \to \mathbb{R}$$

together with a point in the domain of f

$$(t_0, y_0) \in \mathbb{R} \times \mathbb{R},$$

called the _____.

a. ACTRAN
b. ALGOR
c. AUSM
d. Initial condition

6. The _____ is a polynomial mapping of degree 2, often cited as an archetypal example of how complex, chaotic behaviour can arise from very simple non-linear dynamical equations. The map was popularized in a seminal 1976 paper by the biologist Robert May, in part as a discrete-time demographic model analogous to the logistic equation first created by Pierre François Verhulst. Mathematically, the _____ is written

$$(1) \quad x_{n+1} = r x_n (1 - x_n)$$

where:

x_n is a number between zero and one, and represents the population at year n, and hence x_0 represents the initial population (at year 0)

r is a positive number, and represents a combined rate for reproduction and starvation.

a. 15 theorem
b. BDDC
c. Logistic map
d. BIBO stability

7. In mathematics, a _____ (or direction field) is a graphical representation of the solutions of a first-order differential equation. It is achieved without solving the differential equation analytically, and thence it is useful. The representation may be used to qualitatively visualise solutions, or to numerically approximate them.

a. Leibniz function
b. Slope field
c. Visual Calculus
d. Continuous function

8. In mathematics, a (topological) _____ is defined as follows: let I be an interval of real numbers (i.e. a non-empty connected subset of $\mathbb{R}$); then a _____ γ is a continuous mapping $\gamma : I \to X$, where X is a topological space. The _____ γ is said to be simple if it is injective, i.e. if for all x, y in I, we have $\gamma(x) = \gamma(y) \implies x = y$. If I is a closed bounded interval $[a, b]$, we also allow the possibility $\gamma(a) = \gamma(b)$ (this convention makes it possible to talk about closed simple _____.)

Chapter 11. DIFFERENTIAL EQUATIONS

a. Curve
c. Tractrix
b. Prolate cycloid
d. Closed curve

9. In mathematics, an _____ is a generalization for the concept of a function in which the dependent variable has not been given 'explicitly' in terms of the independent variable. To give a function f explicitly is to provide a prescription for determining the output value of the function y in terms of the input value x:

$$y = f(x).$$

By contrast, the function is implicit if the value of y is obtained from x by solving an equation of the form:

$$R(x,y) = 0.$$

a. Implicit differentiation
c. Automatic differentiation
b. Ordinary differential equation
d. Implicit function

10. The _____ is a function in mathematics. The application of this function to a value x is written as exp(x). Equivalently, this can be written in the form e^x, where e is a mathematical constant, the base of the natural logarithm, which equals approximately 2.718281828, and is also known as Euler's number.
a. Exponential function
c. Area hyperbolic functions
b. ACTRAN
d. Integral part

11. _____ (including exponential decay) occurs when the growth rate of a mathematical function is proportional to the function's current value. In the case of a discrete domain of definition with equal intervals it is also called geometric growth or geometric decay (the function values form a geometric progression.)

_____ is said to follow an exponential law; the simple-_____ model is known as the Malthusian growth model.

a. Exponential growth
c. Inseparable differential equation
b. Isomonodromic deformation
d. Oscillating

12. In mathematics, _____ is any of several methods for solving ordinary and partial differential equations, in which algebra allows one to rewrite an equation so that each of two variables occurs on a different side of the equation.

Suppose a differential equation can be written in the form

$$\frac{d}{dx}f(x) = g(x)h(f(x)), \qquad (1)$$

which we can write more simply by letting y = f(x):

$$\frac{dy}{dx} = g(x)h(y).$$

Chapter 11. DIFFERENTIAL EQUATIONS

As long as h(y) ≠ 0, we can rearrange terms to obtain:

$$\frac{dy}{h(y)} = g(x)dx,$$

so that the two variables x and y have been separated.

Some who dislike Leibniz's notation may prefer to write this as

$$\frac{1}{h(y)}\frac{dy}{dx} = g(x),$$

but that fails to make it quite as obvious why this is called '_____'.

a. Power series method
b. Sturm separation theorem
c. Damping ratio
d. Separation of variables

13. A quantity is said to be subject to _____ if it decreases at a rate proportional to its value. Symbolically, this can be expressed as the following differential equation, where N is the quantity and λ is a positive number called the decay constant.

$$\frac{dN}{dt} = -\lambda N.$$

The solution to this equation is:

$$N(t) = N_0 e^{-\lambda t}.$$

Here N(t) is the quantity at time t, and N_0 = N(0) is the initial quantity, i.e. the quantity at time t = 0.

a. ACTRAN
b. Exponential sum
c. ALGOR
d. Exponential decay

14. _____ is the concept of adding accumulated interest back to the principal, so that interest is earned on interest from that moment on. The act of declaring interest to be principal is called compounding (i.e., interest is compounded.) A loan, for example, may have its interest compounded every month: in this case, a loan with $100 principal and 1% interest per month would have a balance of $101 at the end of the first month.

a. BIBO stability
b. BDDC
c. Compound interest
d. 15 theorem

15. The _____ of a quantity whose value decreases with time is the interval required for the quantity to decay to half of its initial value. The concept originated in describing how long it takes atoms to undergo radioactive decay but also applies in a wide variety of other situations.

Chapter 11. DIFFERENTIAL EQUATIONS

The term '_____' dates to 1907.

a. BIBO stability
b. 15 theorem
c. Half-life
d. BDDC

16. The _____ are a pair of first order, non-linear, differential equations frequently used to describe the dynamics of biological systems in which two species interact, one a predator and one its prey. They were proposed independently by Alfred J. Lotka in 1925 and Vito Volterra in 1926.

where

- y is the number of some predator;
- x is the number of its prey;
- dy/dt and dx/dt represents the growth of the two populations against time;
- t represents the time; and
- >α, >β, >γ and >δ are parameters representing the interaction of the two species.

When multiplied out, the equations take a form useful for physical interpretation. Their origin should be considered from a more general framework,

where both functions represent per capita growth rates of the prey and predator, respectively.

a. Lotka-Volterra equations
b. BDDC
c. 15 theorem
d. BIBO stability

17. In physics, _____ is defined as the rate of change of position. it is vector physical quantity; both speed and direction are required to define it. In the SI (metric) system, it is measured in meters per second: (m/s) or ms^{-1}.

a. BIBO stability
b. 15 theorem
c. BDDC
d. Velocity

18. In physics, _____ is the speed where the kinetic energy of an object is equal to the magnitude of its gravitational potential energy, as calculated by the equation,

Chapter 11. DIFFERENTIAL EQUATIONS

$$U_g = \frac{-Gm_1 m_2}{r}.$$

It is commonly described as the speed needed to 'break free' from a gravitational field (without any additional impulse.) The term _____ can be considered a misnomer because it is actually a speed rather than a velocity, i.e. it specifies how fast the object must move but the direction of movement is irrelevant, unless 'downward.' In more technical terms, _____ is a scalar (and not a vector.)

The phenomenon of _____ is a consequence of conservation of energy.

a. ACTRAN
b. AUSM
c. Escape velocity
d. ALGOR

19. A _____ is a visual display of certain characteristics of certain kinds of differential equations.

Phase planes are useful in visualizing the behavior of physical systems; in particular, of oscillatory systems such as predator-prey models These models can 'spiral in' towards zero, 'spiral out' towards infinity, or reach neutrally stable situations called centres where the path traced out can be either circular, elliptical, or ovoid, or some variant thereof.

a. Spectral theory of ordinary differential equations
b. Boundary value problem
c. Node
d. Phase plane

20. In mathematics, the point $\tilde{\mathbf{x}} \in \mathbb{R}^n$ is an _____ for the differential equation

$$\frac{d\mathbf{x}}{dt} = \mathbf{f}(t, \mathbf{x})$$

if $\mathbf{f}(t, \tilde{\mathbf{x}}) = 0$ for all t.

Similarly, the point $\tilde{\mathbf{x}} \in \mathbb{R}^n$ is an _____ (or fixed point) for the difference equation

$$\mathbf{x}_{k+1} = \mathbf{f}(k, \mathbf{x}_k)$$

if $\mathbf{f}(k, \tilde{\mathbf{x}}) = \tilde{\mathbf{x}}$ for $k = 0, 1, 2, \ldots$.

Equilibria can be classified by looking at the signs of the eigenvalues of the linearization of the equations about the equilibria.

Chapter 11. DIFFERENTIAL EQUATIONS

a. AUSM
b. ACTRAN
c. Equilibrium point
d. ALGOR

21. A curve γ is said to be closed or a loop if $I = [a, b]$ and if $\gamma(a) = \gamma(b)$. A _____ is thus a continuous mapping of the circle S^1; a simple _____ is also called a Jordan curve or a Jordan arc. The Jordan curve theorem states that such curves divide the plane into an 'interior' and an 'exterior'.

a. Curve
b. Kappa curve
c. Bullet-nose curve
d. Closed curve

22. Nullclines, sometimes called zero-growth isoclines (which were developed by MIT mathematicians in early 20th century), are encountered in two-dimensional systems of differential equations

x' = F(x,y)
y' = G(x,y.)

They are curves along which the vector field is either completely horizontal or vertical. A _____ is a boundary between regions where x' or y' switch signs. Nullclines can be found by setting either x' = 0 or y' = 0.

a. Riemann-Hilbert correspondence
b. Delay differential equation
c. Homogeneous differential equation
d. Nullcline

23. In mathematics, in the field of ordinary differential equations, a non trivial solution to an ordinary differential equation

$$F(x, y, y', \ldots, y^{(n-1)}) = y^{(n)} \quad x \in [0, +\infty)$$

is called _____ if it has an infinite number of roots, otherwise it is called non-_____. The differential equation is called _____ if it has an _____ solution.

The differential equation

y" + y = 0

is _____ as sin(x) is a solution.

a. Integrating factor
b. Oscillating
c. Exponential growth
d. Inseparable differential equation

24. The most commonly encountered form of Hooke's law is probably the spring equation, which relates the force exerted by a spring to the distance it is stretched by a _____, k, measured in force per length.

$$F = -kx$$

The negative sign indicates that the force exerted by the spring is in direct opposition to the direction of displacement. It is called a 'restoring force', as it tends to restore the system to equilibrium.

Chapter 11. DIFFERENTIAL EQUATIONS

  a. Spring equation
  c. Polar moment of inertia
  b. Spring constant
  d. Navier-Stokes equations

25. In acoustics and telecommunication, a _____ of a wave is a component frequency of the signal that is an integer multiple of the fundamental frequency. For example, if the fundamental frequency is f, the harmonics have frequencies f, 2f, 3f, 4f, etc. The harmonics have the property that they are all periodic at the fundamental frequency, therefore the sum of harmonics is also periodic at that frequency.
  a. BDDC
  c. BIBO stability
  b. 15 theorem
  d. Harmonic

26. _____ is the motion of a simple harmonic oscillator, a motion that is neither driven nor damped. The motion is periodic - as it repeats itself at standard intervals in a specific manner - and sinusoidal, with constant amplitude; the acceleration of a body executing _____ is directly proportional to the displacement of the body from the equilibrium position and is always directed towards the equilibrium position.

The motion is characterized by its amplitude (which is always positive), its period, the time for a single oscillation, its frequency, the reciprocal of the period (i.e. the number of cycles per unit time), and its phase, which determines the starting point on the sine wave.

  a. Fundamental lemma in the calculus of variations
  c. Holonomic
  b. 15 theorem
  d. Simple harmonic Motion

27. Trigonometry is a branch of mathematics that deals with triangles, particularly those plane triangles in which one angle has 90 degrees (right triangles.) Trigonometry deals with relationships between the sides and the angles of triangles and with the _____ functions, which describe those relationships.

Trigonometry has applications in both pure mathematics and in applied mathematics, where it is essential in many branches of science and technology.

  a. Trigonometric functions
  c. Sine
  b. Trigonometric integrals
  d. Trigonometric

28. In mathematics, the _____ are functions of an angle. They are important in the study of triangles and modeling periodic phenomena, among many other applications. _____ are commonly defined as ratios of two sides of a right triangle containing the angle, and can equivalently be defined as the lengths of various line segments from a unit circle.
  a. Trigonometric
  c. Sine integral
  b. Trigonometric integrals
  d. Trigonometric functions

29. The _____ of an angle is the ratio of the length of the opposite side to the length of the hypotenuse. In our case

$$\sin A = \frac{\text{opposite}}{\text{hypotenuse}} = \frac{a}{h}.$$

Note that this ratio does not depend on size of the particular right triangle chosen, as long as it contains the angle A, since all such triangles are similar.

Chapter 11. DIFFERENTIAL EQUATIONS

The cosine of an angle is the ratio of the length of the adjacent side to the length of the hypotenuse.

a. Trigonometric functions
b. Trigonometric
c. Sine
d. Sine integral

30. In physics, _____ is movement that changes the position of an object, as opposed to rotation. For example, according to Whittaker:

A _____ is the operation changing the positions of all points (x, y, z) of an object according to the formula

$$(x, y, z) \rightarrow (x + \Delta x, y + \Delta y, z + \Delta z)$$

where $(\Delta x, \Delta y, \Delta z)$ is the same vector for each point of the object. The _____ vector $(\Delta x, \Delta y, \Delta z)$ common to all points of the object describes a particular type of displacement of the object, usually called a linear displacement to distinguish it from displacements involving rotation, called angular displacements.

a. 15 theorem
b. BIBO stability
c. BDDC
d. Translation

31. _____ is any effect, either deliberately engendered or inherent to a system, that tends to reduce the amplitude of oscillations of an oscillatory system.

In physics and engineering, _____ may be mathematically modelled as a force synchronous with the velocity of the object but opposite in direction to it. If such force is also proportional to the velocity, as for a simple mechanical viscous damper (dashpot), the force F may be related to the velocity v by

$$\mathbf{F} = -c\mathbf{v}$$

where c is the viscous _____ coefficient, given in units of newton-seconds per meter.

a. 15 theorem
b. BIBO stability
c. BDDC
d. Damping

32. In mathematics, a _____ is a constant multiplicative factor of a certain object. For example, in the expression $9x^2$, the _____ of x^2 is 9.

The object can be such things as a variable, a vector, a function, etc.

a. Resultant
b. Degree of the polynomial
c. Binomial type
d. Coefficient

33. In mathematics, the complex numbers are an extension of the real numbers obtained by adjoining an imaginary unit, denoted i.

Every _____ can be written in the form a + bi, where a and b are real numbers called the real part and the imaginary part of the _____, respectively.

Complex numbers are a field, and thus have addition, subtraction, multiplication, and division operations. These operations extend the corresponding operations on real numbers, although with a number of additional elegant and useful properties, e.g., negative real numbers can be obtained by squaring complex (imaginary) numbers.

a. Real part
c. Conjugated line
b. Complex number
d. Filled Julia set

34. Integration is an important concept in mathematics, specifically in the field of calculus and, more broadly, mathematical analysis. Given a function f of a real variable x and an interval [a, b] of the real line, the _____

$$\int_a^b f(x)\,dx,$$

is defined informally to be the net signed area of the region in the xy-plane bounded by the graph of f, the x-axis, and the vertical lines x = a and x = b.

The term '_____' may also refer to the notion of antiderivative, a function F whose derivative is the given function f.

a. Integrand
c. Integral test for convergence
b. Integral
d. Indefinite integral

Chapter 12. FUNCTIONS OF SEVERAL VARIABLES

1. In economics, the _____ functional form of production functions is widely used to represent the relationship of an output to inputs. It was proposed by Knut Wicksell (1851-1926), and tested against statistical evidence by Charles Cobb and Paul Douglas in 1900-1928.

For production, the function is

$$Y = AL^{\alpha}K^{\beta},$$

where:

- Y = total production (the monetary value of all goods produced in a year)
- L = labor input
- K = capital input
- A = total factor productivity
- α and β are the output elasticities of labor and capital, respectively. These values are constants determined by available technology.

Output elasticity measures the responsiveness of output to a change in levels of either labor or capital used in production, ceteris paribus. For example if α = 0.15, a 1% increase in labor would lead to approximately a 0.15% increase in output.

a. BDDC
b. 15 theorem
c. BIBO stability
d. Cobb-Douglas

2. The terms '_____' and 'independent variable' are used in similar but subtly different ways in mathematics and statistics as part of the standard terminology in those subjects. They are used to distinguish between two types of quantities being considered, separating them into those available at the start of a process and those being created by it, where the latter (dependent variables) are dependent on the former (independent variables.)

In traditional calculus, a function is defined as a relation between two terms called variables because their values vary.

a. 15 theorem
b. BIBO stability
c. Dependent variable
d. BDDC

3. The terms 'dependent variable' and '_____' are used in similar but subtly different ways in mathematics and statistics as part of the standard terminology in those subjects. They are used to distinguish between two types of quantities being considered, separating them into those available at the start of a process and those being created by it, where the latter (dependent variables) are dependent on the former (independent variables.)

In traditional calculus, a function is defined as a relation between two terms called variables because their values vary.

a. ACTRAN
b. Independent variable
c. AUSM
d. ALGOR

Chapter 12. FUNCTIONS OF SEVERAL VARIABLES

4. The _____, L, of a dynamical system is a function that summarizes the dynamics of the system. It is named after Joseph Louis Lagrange. The concept of a _____ was originally introduced in a reformulation of classical mechanics known as _____ mechanics.
   a. Klein-Gordon equation
   b. Lagrangian
   c. Dirac equation
   d. Vector potential

5. In mathematics, the _____ is a representation of a function as an infinite sum of terms calculated from the values of its derivatives at a single point. It may be regarded as the limit of the Taylor polynomials. If the series is centered at zero, the series is also called a Maclaurin series.
   a. BDDC
   b. BIBO stability
   c. 15 theorem
   d. Taylor series

6. In mathematics and its applications, a _____ system is a system for assigning an n-tuple of numbers or scalars to each point in an n-dimensional space. This concept is part of the theory of manifolds. 'Scalars' in many cases means real numbers, but, depending on context, can mean complex numbers or elements of some other commutative ring.
   a. Cylindrical coordinate system
   b. Spherical coordinate system
   c. 15 theorem
   d. Coordinate

7. A _____ is one of the most curvilinear basic geometric shapes:It has two faces, zero vertices, and zero edges. The surface formed by the points at a fixed distance from a given straight line, the axis of the _____. The solid enclosed by this surface and by two planes perpendicular to the axis is also called a _____.
   a. BDDC
   b. Right circular cylinder
   c. 15 theorem
   d. Cylinder

8. In mathematics, the hyperbolic functions are analogs of the ordinary trigonometric functions. The basic hyperbolic functions are the hyperbolic sine 'sinh', and the _____ 'cosh', from which are derived the hyperbolic tangent 'tanh', etc., in analogy to the derived trigonometric functions. The inverse hyperbolic functions are the area hyperbolic sine 'arsinh' (also called 'asinh', or sometimes by the misnomer of 'arcsinh') and so on.
   a. Hyperbolic cosine
   b. Step function
   c. Square root function
   d. Hyperbolic tangent

9. _____ generally conveys two primary meanings. The first is an imprecise sense of harmonious or aesthetically-pleasing proportionality and balance; such that it reflects beauty or perfection. The second meaning is a precise and well-defined concept of balance or 'patterned self-similarity' that can be demonstrated or proved according to the rules of a formal system: by geometry, through physics or otherwise.
   a. BIBO stability
   b. 15 theorem
   c. BDDC
   d. Symmetry

10. A _____ is perfectly round geometrical object in three-dimensional space, such as the shape of a round ball. Like a circle in two dimensions, a perfect _____ is completely symmetrical around its center, with all points on the surface lying the same distance r from the center point. This distance r is known as the radius of the _____.
    a. North pole
    b. Tangent line
    c. Sphere
    d. Minimal surface

11. In mathematics, a _____ is a quadric surface of special kind. There are two kinds of paraboloids: elliptic and hyperbolic. The elliptic _____ is shaped like an oval cup and can have a maximum or minimum point.

Chapter 12. FUNCTIONS OF SEVERAL VARIABLES

a. Torus
b. Hyperbolic paraboloid
c. Paraboloid
d. PDE surfaces

12. A _____ is a surface created by rotating a curve lying on some plane (the generatrix) around a straight line (the axis of rotation) that lies on the same plane.

Examples of surfaces generated by a straight line are the cylindrical and conical surfaces. A circle that is rotated about a (coplanar) axis through the center generates a sphere.

a. Surface of revolution
b. Constant of integration
c. Shell integration
d. Riemann sum

13. A _____ of a function of two variables is a curve along which the function has a constant value. In cartography, a _____ (often just called a 'contour') joins points of equal elevation (height) above a given level, such as mean sea level. A contour map is a map illustrated with contour lines, for example a topographic map, which thus shows valleys and hills, and the steepness of slopes.

a. BDDC
b. 15 theorem
c. BIBO stability
d. Contour line

14. In mathematics, a (topological) _____ is defined as follows: let I be an interval of real numbers (i.e. a non-empty connected subset of $\mathbb{R}$); then a _____ γ is a continuous mapping $\gamma : I \to X$, where X is a topological space. The _____ γ is said to be simple if it is injective, i.e. if for all x, y in I, we have $\gamma(x) = \gamma(y) \implies x = y$. If I is a closed bounded interval $[a, b]$, we also allow the possibility $\gamma(a) = \gamma(b)$ (this convention makes it possible to talk about closed simple _____.)

a. Tractrix
b. Closed curve
c. Curve
d. Prolate cycloid

15. When the number of variables is two, this is a _____, if it is three this is a level surface, and for higher values of n the level set is a level hypersurface.

More specifically, a _____ is the set of all real-valued roots of an equation in two variables x_1 and x_2. A level surface is the set of all real-valued roots of an equation in three variables x_1, x_2 and x_3.

a. Multipole moment
b. Scalar field
c. Level curve
d. Partial derivative

16. In mathematics, a _____ is a point in the domain of a function of two variables which is a stationary point but not a local extremum. At such a point, in general, the surface resembles a saddle that curves up in one direction, and curves down in a different direction (like a mountain pass.) In terms of contour lines, a _____ can be recognized, in general, by a contour that appears to intersect itself.

a. 15 theorem
b. BDDC
c. Saddle point
d. BIBO stability

17. In mathematics, _____ and minima, known collectively as extrema, are the largest value (maximum) or smallest value (minimum), that a function takes in a point either within a given neighbourhood (local extremum) or on the function domain in its entirety (global extremum.)

Throughout, a point refers to an input (x), while a value refers to an output (y): one distinguishing between the maximum value and the point (or points) at which it occurs.

A real-valued function f defined on the real line is said to have a local maximum point at the point x^*, if there exists some $\varepsilon > 0$, such that $f(x^*) \geq f(x)$ when $|x - x^*| < \varepsilon$.

a. Racetrack principle
c. Maxima
b. Leibniz formula
d. Related rates

18. In mathematics, a hyperboloid is a quadric, a type of surface in three dimensions, described by the equation

$$\frac{x^2}{a^2} + \frac{y^2}{b^2} - \frac{z^2}{c^2} = 1 \quad \underline{\qquad},$$

or

$$-\frac{x^2}{a^2} - \frac{y^2}{b^2} + \frac{z^2}{c^2} = 1 \quad \text{hyperboloid of two sheets.}$$

These are also called elliptical hyperboloids. If, and only if, a = b, it is a hyperboloid of revolution, and is also called a circular hyperboloid.

a. BDDC
c. BIBO stability
b. 15 theorem
d. Hyperboloid of one sheet

19. A _____ is a lens which focuses light which passes through onto a line instead of onto a point, as a spherical lens would. The curved face or faces of a _____ are sections of a cylinder, and focus the image passing through it onto a line parallel to the intersection of the surface of the lens and a plane tangent to it. The lens compresses the image in the direction perpendicular to this line, and leaves it unaltered in the direction parallel to it (in the tangent plane.)

a. BDDC
c. BIBO stability
b. 15 theorem
d. Cylindrical lens

20. In mathematics, the concept of a '_____' is used to describe the behavior of a function as its argument or input either 'gets close' to some point, or as the argument becomes arbitrarily large; or the behavior of a sequence's elements as their index increases indefinitely. Limits are used in calculus and other branches of mathematical analysis to define derivatives and continuity.

In formulas, _____ is usually abbreviated as lim

a. BIBO stability
b. 15 theorem
c. Limit
d. BDDC

Chapter 13. A FUNDAMENTAL TOOL: VECTORS

1. In elementary mathematics, physics, and engineering, a _____ is a geometric object that has both a magnitude (or length), direction and sense, (i.e., orientation along the given direction.) A _____ is frequently represented by a line segment with a definite direction, or graphically as an arrow, connecting an initial point A with a terminal point B, and denoted by

The magnitude of the _____ is the length of the segment and the direction characterizes the displacement of B relative to A: how much one should move the point A to 'carry' it to the point B.

Many algebraic operations on real numbers have close analogues for vectors.

a. 15 theorem
b. BDDC
c. Linear partial differential operator
d. Vector

2. In physics, _____ is movement that changes the position of an object, as opposed to rotation. For example, according to Whittaker:

A _____ is the operation changing the positions of all points (x, y, z) of an object according to the formula

$$(x, y, z) \rightarrow (x + \Delta x, y + \Delta y, z + \Delta z)$$

where $(\Delta x, \Delta y, \Delta z)$ is the same vector for each point of the object. The _____ vector $(\Delta x, \Delta y, \Delta z)$ common to all points of the object describes a particular type of displacement of the object, usually called a linear displacement to distinguish it from displacements involving rotation, called angular displacements.

a. 15 theorem
b. Translation
c. BDDC
d. BIBO stability

3. In mathematics, _____ is one of the basic operations defining a vector space in linear algebra Note that _____ is different from scalar product which is an inner product between two vectors.

More specifically, if K is a field and V is a vector space over K, then _____ is a function from K × V to V. The result of applying this function to c in K and v in V is denoted cv.

a. Vector-valued function
b. Homogeneous function
c. Direction cosines
d. Scalar multiplication

4. In linear algebra, the null vector or _____ is the vector (0, 0, …, 0) in Euclidean space, all of whose components are zero. It is usually written $\vec{0}$ or 0 or simply 0. A _____ has no direction.

a. Scalar multiplication
b. Zero vector
c. Direction vector
d. Homogeneous function

Chapter 13. A FUNDAMENTAL TOOL: VECTORS

5. In mathematics, a _____ in a normed vector space is a vector (often a spatial vector) whose length is 1 (the unit length.) A _____ is often denoted by a lowercase letter with a superscribed caret or e;hate;, like this: $\hat{\imath}$.

In Euclidean space, the dot product of two unit vectors is simply the cosine of the angle between them.

a. Unit vector
b. Overdetermined
c. ACTRAN
d. ALGOR

6. In mathematics, a (topological) _____ is defined as follows: let I be an interval of real numbers (i.e. a non-empty connected subset of $\mathbb{R}$); then a _____ γ is a continuous mapping $\gamma : I \to X$, where X is a topological space. The _____ γ is said to be simple if it is injective, i.e. if for all x, y in I, we have $\gamma(x) = \gamma(y) \implies x = y$. If I is a closed bounded interval $[a, b]$, we also allow the possibility $\gamma(a) = \gamma(b)$ (this convention makes it possible to talk about closed simple _____.)

a. Closed curve
b. Prolate cycloid
c. Tractrix
d. Curve

7. In physics, _____ is defined as the rate of change of position. it is vector physical quantity; both speed and direction are required to define it. In the SI (metric) system, it is measured in meters per second: (m/s) or ms^{-1}.

a. BIBO stability
b. 15 theorem
c. BDDC
d. Velocity

8. In physics, and more specifically kinematics, _____ is the change in velocity over time. Because velocity is a vector, it can change in two ways: a change in magnitude and/or a change in direction. In one dimension, _____ is the rate at which something speeds up or slows down.

a. ACTRAN
b. Acceleration
c. ALGOR
d. AUSM

9. In mathematics and its applications, a _____ system is a system for assigning an n-tuple of numbers or scalars to each point in an n-dimensional space. This concept is part of the theory of manifolds. 'Scalars' in many cases means real numbers, but, depending on context, can mean complex numbers or elements of some other commutative ring.

a. 15 theorem
b. Cylindrical coordinate system
c. Spherical coordinate system
d. Coordinate

10. In mathematics, an _____ space is a topological space whose dimension is n (where n is a fixed natural number.) The archetypical example is _____ Euclidean space, which describes Euclidean geometry in n dimensions.

Many familiar geometric objects can be generalized to any number of dimensions.

a. BDDC
b. N-dimensional
c. BIBO stability
d. 15 theorem

11. In mathematics, the _____ is an operation which takes two vectors over the real numbers R and returns a real-valued scalar quantity. It is the standard inner product of the orthonormal Euclidean space. It contrasts with the cross product which produces a vector result.

a. Homogeneous function
c. Vector-valued function
b. Dot product
d. Scalar multiplication

12. In mathematics, two vectors are _____ if they are perpendicular, i.e., they form a right angle. For example, a subway and the street above, although they do not physically intersect, are _____ if they cross at a right angle.
   a. ACTRAN
   c. AUSM
   b. Orthogonal
   d. ALGOR

13. A surface normal to a flat surface is a vector which is perpendicular to that surface. A normal to a non-flat surface at a point P on the surface is a vector perpendicular to the tangent plane to that surface at P. The word 'normal' is also used as an adjective: a line normal to a plane, the normal component of a force, the _____, etc. The concept of normality generalizes to orthogonality.
   a. Normal vector
   c. Hyperbolic paraboloid
   b. Paraboloid
   d. Normal line

14. The vector resolute (also known as the _____) of two vectors, $\mathbf{a}$ in the direction of $\mathbf{b}$ (also '$\mathbf{a}$ on $\mathbf{b}$'), is given by:

$$(\mathbf{a} \cdot \hat{\mathbf{b}})\hat{\mathbf{b}} \text{ or } (|\mathbf{a}|\cos\theta)\hat{\mathbf{b}}$$

where θ is the angle between the vectors $\mathbf{b}$ and $\mathbf{a}$ and $\hat{\mathbf{b}}$ is the unit vector in the direction of $\mathbf{b}$.

The vector resolute is a vector, and is the orthogonal projection of the vector $\mathbf{a}$ onto the vector $\mathbf{b}$. The vector resolute is also said to be a component of vector $\mathbf{a}$ in the direction of vector $\mathbf{b}$.

   a. BIBO stability
   c. Vector projection
   b. 15 theorem
   d. BDDC

15. In mathematics and physics, the _____ is a common mnemonic for understanding notation conventions for vectors in 3 dimensions. It was invented for use in electromagnetism by British physicist Zachariah William Cole in the late 1800s.

When choosing three vectors that must be at right angles to each other, there are two distinct solutions, so when expressing this idea in mathematics, one must remove the ambiguity of which solution is meant.

   a. Right-hand rule
   c. 15 theorem
   b. BDDC
   d. BIBO stability

16. Integration is an important concept in mathematics, specifically in the field of calculus and, more broadly, mathematical analysis. Given a function f of a real variable x and an interval [a, b] of the real line, the _____

$$\int_a^b f(x)\,dx,$$

is defined informally to be the net signed area of the region in the xy-plane bounded by the graph of f, the x-axis, and the vertical lines x = a and x = b.

The term '_____' may also refer to the notion of antiderivative, a function F whose derivative is the given function f.

a. Indefinite integral
b. Integrand
c. Integral test for convergence
d. Integral

17. In vector calculus, the _____ is shorthand for either the _____ matrix or its determinant, the _____ determinant.

In algebraic geometry the _____ of a curve means the _____ variety: a group variety associated to the curve, in which the curve can be embedded.

These concepts are all named after the mathematician Carl Gustav Jacob Jacobi.

a. Saddle surface
b. Critical point
c. Vector Laplacian
d. Jacobian

18. In geometry, a _____ is a three-dimensional figure formed by six parallelograms. It is to a parallelogram as a cube is to a square: Euclidean geometry supports all four notions but affine geometry admits only parallelograms and parallelepipeds. Three equivalent definitions of _____ are

- a polyhedron with six faces (hexahedron), each of which is a parallelogram,
- a hexahedron with three pairs of parallel faces, and
- a prism of which the base is a parallelogram.

The cuboid (six rectangular faces), cube (six square faces), and the rhombohedron (six rhombus faces) are all specific cases of _____.

Parallelepipeds are a subclass of the prismatoids.

a. BIBO stability
b. 15 theorem
c. BDDC
d. Parallelepiped

19. In geometry, for a finite planar surface of scalar area S, the _____

S

is defined as a vector whose magnitude is S and whose direction is perpendicular to the plane, as determined by the right hand rule on the rim (moving one's right hand counterclockwise around the rim, when the palm of the hand is 'touching' the surface, and the straight thumb indicate the direction.)

$$\mathbf{S} = \hat{\mathbf{n}} S$$

This can only be defined for flat surfaces, or for regions of curved surfaces which are sufficiently small that they can be considered flat.

The concept of an area vector simplifies the equation for determining the flux through the surface.

a. Surface area
b. Vector area
c. Lipschitz domain
d. Gyroid

20. In geometry, for a finite planar surface of scalar area S, the vector area

$$\mathbf{S}$$

is defined as a vector whose magnitude is S and whose direction is perpendicular to the plane, as determined by the right hand rule on the rim (moving one's right hand counterclockwise around the rim, when the palm of the hand is 'touching' the surface, and the straight thumb indicate the direction.)

$$\mathbf{S} = \hat{\mathbf{n}} S$$

This can only be defined for flat surfaces, or for regions of curved surfaces which are sufficiently small that they can be considered flat.

The concept of an _____ simplifies the equation for determining the flux through the surface.

a. ALGOR
b. ACTRAN
c. Orthogonal trajectories
d. Area Vector

Chapter 14. DIFFERENTIATING FUNCTIONS OF SEVERAL VARIABLES

1. In calculus, a branch of mathematics, the _____ is a measurement of how a function changes when its input changes. Loosely speaking, a _____ can be thought of as how much a quantity is changing at some given point. For example, the _____ of the position (or distance) of a vehicle with respect to time is the instantaneous velocity (respectively, instantaneous speed) at which the vehicle is traveling.

The process of finding a _____ is called differentiation. The fundamental theorem of calculus states that differentiation is the reverse process to integration.

    a. Bounded function   b. Derivative
    c. Semi-differentiability   d. Stationary phase approximation

2. In mathematics, a _____ of a function of several variables is its derivative with respect to one of those variables with the others held constant (as opposed to the total derivative, in which all variables are allowed to vary.) Partial derivatives are useful in vector calculus and differential geometry.

The _____ of a function f with respect to the variable x is written as f'_x, $\partial_x f$, or $\partial f/\partial x$.

    a. Jacobian   b. Differentiation operator
    c. Level curve   d. Partial derivative

3. The function difference divided by the point difference is known as the _____, it is also known as Newton's quotient):

$$\frac{\Delta F(P)}{\Delta P} = \frac{F(P + \Delta P) - F(P)}{\Delta P} = \frac{\nabla F(P + \Delta P)}{\Delta P}.$$

If ΔP is infinitesimal, then the _____ is a derivative, otherwise it is a divided difference:

$$\text{If } |\Delta P| = iota: \quad \frac{\Delta F(P)}{\Delta P} = \frac{dF(P)}{dP} = F'(P) = G(P);$$

$$\text{If } |\Delta P| > iota: \quad \frac{\Delta F(P)}{\Delta P} = \frac{DF(P)}{DP} = F[P, P + \Delta P].$$

Regardless if ΔP is infinitesimal or finite, there is (at least--in the case of the derivative--theoretically) a point range, where the boundaries are P ± (.5)ΔP (depending on the orientation--ΔF(P), δF(P) or ∇F(P)):

        LB = Lower Boundary; UB = Upper Boundary;

Anyone familiar with derivatives knows that they can be regarded as functions themselves, harboring their own derivatives. Thus each function is home to sequential degrees ('higher orders') of derivation, or differentiation. This property can be generalized to all difference quotients. As this sequencing requires a corresponding boundary splintering, it is practical to break up the point range into smaller, equi-sized sections, with each section being marked by an intermediary point ('P_i'), where LB = P_0 and UB = P_{A_n}, the nth point, equaling the degree/order:

Chapter 14. DIFFERENTIATING FUNCTIONS OF SEVERAL VARIABLES

$LB = P_0 = P_0 + 0\Delta_1 P = P_{A_n} - (Åf\text{-}0)\Delta_1 P$; $P_1 = P_0 + 1\Delta_1 P = P_{A_n} - (Åf\text{-}1)\Delta_1 P$; $P_2 = P_0 + 2\Delta_1 P = P_{A_n} - (Åf\text{-}2)\Delta_1 P$; $P_3 = P_0 + 3\Delta_1 P = P_{A_n} - (Åf\text{-}3)\Delta_1 P$; $\downarrow\downarrow\downarrow\downarrow P_{A_n\text{-}3} = P_0 + (Åf\text{-}3)\Delta_1 P = P_{A_n} - 3\Delta_1 P$; $P_{A_n\text{-}2} = P_0 + (Åf\text{-}2)\Delta_1 P = P_{A_n} - 2\Delta_1 P$; $P_{A_n\text{-}1} = P_0 + (Åf\text{-}1)\Delta_1 P = P_{A_n} - 1\Delta_1 P$; $UB = P_{A_n\text{-}0} = P_0 + (Åf\text{-}0)\Delta_1 P = P_{A_n} - 0\Delta_1 P = P_{A_n}$;

$\Delta P = \Delta_1 P = P_1 - P_0 = P_2 - P_1 = P_3 - P_2 = \ldots$

a. Directional derivative
b. Continuously differentiable
c. Notation for differentiation
d. Difference quotient

4. In economics, the _____ functional form of production functions is widely used to represent the relationship of an output to inputs. It was proposed by Knut Wicksell (1851-1926), and tested against statistical evidence by Charles Cobb and Paul Douglas in 1900-1928.

For production, the function is

$$Y = AL^\alpha K^\beta,$$

where:

- Y = total production (the monetary value of all goods produced in a year)
- L = labor input
- K = capital input
- A = total factor productivity
- α and β are the output elasticities of labor and capital, respectively. These values are constants determined by available technology.

Output elasticity measures the responsiveness of output to a change in levels of either labor or capital used in production, ceteris paribus. For example if $\alpha = 0.15$, a 1% increase in labor would lead to approximately a 0.15% increase in output.

a. 15 theorem
b. Cobb-Douglas
c. BIBO stability
d. BDDC

5. In mathematics, the hyperbolic functions are analogs of the ordinary trigonometric functions. The basic hyperbolic functions are the hyperbolic sine 'sinh', and the _____ 'cosh', from which are derived the hyperbolic tangent 'tanh', etc., in analogy to the derived trigonometric functions. The inverse hyperbolic functions are the area hyperbolic sine 'arsinh' (also called 'asinh', or sometimes by the misnomer of 'arcsinh') and so on.

a. Hyperbolic cosine
b. Square root function
c. Step function
d. Hyperbolic tangent

Chapter 14. DIFFERENTIATING FUNCTIONS OF SEVERAL VARIABLES

6. _____ generally conveys two primary meanings. The first is an imprecise sense of harmonious or aesthetically-pleasing proportionality and balance; such that it reflects beauty or perfection. The second meaning is a precise and well-defined concept of balance or 'patterned self-similarity' that can be demonstrated or proved according to the rules of a formal system: by geometry, through physics or otherwise.
   - a. BIBO stability
   - b. BDDC
   - c. 15 theorem
   - d. Symmetry

7. In mathematics and its applications, _____ refers to finding the linear approximation to a function at a given point. In the study of dynamical systems, _____ is a method for assessing the local stability of an equilibrium point of a system of nonlinear differential equations or discrete dynamical systems. This method is used in fields such as engineering, physics, economics, and ecology.
   - a. Differentiation of trigonometric functions
   - b. Parametric derivative
   - c. Smooth function
   - d. Linearization

8. In geometry, the _____ (or simply the tangent) to a curve at a given point is the straight line that 'just touches' the curve at that point (in the sense explained more precisely below.) As it passes through the point of tangency, the _____ is 'going in the same direction' as the curve, and in this sense it is the best straight-line approximation to the curve at that point. The same definition applies to space curves and curves in n-dimensional Euclidean space.
   - a. North pole
   - b. Tangent line
   - c. Lie derivative
   - d. Minimal surface

9. In mathematics, the interior of a set S consists of all points of S that are intuitively 'not on the edge of S'. A point that is in the interior of S is an _____ of S.

   The exterior of a set is the interior of its complement; it consists of the points that are not in the set or its boundary.
   - a. ALGOR
   - b. Interior Point
   - c. AUSM
   - d. ACTRAN

10. In infinitesimal calculus, a _____ is traditionally an infinitesimally small change in a variable. For example, if x is a variable, then a change in the value of x is often denoted Δx (or δx when this change is considered to be small.) The _____ dx represents such a change, but is infinitely small.
    - a. Local maximum
    - b. The Method of Mechanical Theorems
    - c. Differential
    - d. Dirichlet integral

11. The _____ is the equation of state of a hypothetical ideal gas, first stated by Benoît Paul Émile Clapeyron in 1834. The law is derived from the fact that in the ideal state of any gas a given number of its 'particles' occupy the same volume, and that volume changes are inverse to pressure changes and linear to temperature changes.

    The state of an amount of gas is determined by its pressure, volume, and temperature according to the equation:

    $$pV = nRT$$

where

p is the absolute pressure of the gas,
V is the volume of the gas,
n is the number of moles of gas,
R is the universal gas constant,
T is the absolute temperature.

a. ACTRAN
b. AUSM
c. Ideal gas law
d. ALGOR

12. In mathematics, the _____ of a multivariate differentiable function along a given vector V at a given point P intuitively represents the instantaneous rate of change of the function, moving through P, in the direction of V. It therefore generalizes the notion of a partial derivative, in which the direction is always taken parallel to one of the coordinate axes.

The _____ is a special case of the Gâteaux derivative.

The _____ of a scalar function $f(\vec{x}) = f(x_1, x_2, \ldots, x_n)$ along a vector $\vec{v} = (v_1, \ldots, v_n)$ is the function defined by the limit

$$\nabla_{\vec{v}} f(\vec{x}) = \lim_{h \to 0} \frac{f(\vec{x} + h\vec{v}) - f(\vec{x})}{h}.$$

Sometimes authors write D_v instead of ∇_v.

a. Symmetrically continuous
b. Differentiation of trigonometric functions
c. Linearity of differentiation
d. Directional derivative

13. In vector calculus, the _____ of a scalar field is a vector field which points in the direction of the greatest rate of increase of the scalar field, and whose magnitude is the greatest rate of change.

A generalization of the _____ for functions on a Euclidean space which have values in another Euclidean space is the Jacobian. A further generalization for a function from one Banach space to another is the Fréchet derivative.

a. Symmetric derivative
b. Lin-Tsien equation
c. Smooth function
d. Gradient

14. In elementary mathematics, physics, and engineering, a _____ is a geometric object that has both a magnitude (or length), direction and sense, (i.e., orientation along the given direction.) A _____ is frequently represented by a line segment with a definite direction, or graphically as an arrow, connecting an initial point A with a terminal point B, and denoted by

Chapter 14. DIFFERENTIATING FUNCTIONS OF SEVERAL VARIABLES

The magnitude of the _____ is the length of the segment and the direction characterizes the displacement of B relative to A: how much one should move the point A to 'carry' it to the point B.

Many algebraic operations on real numbers have close analogues for vectors.

a. 15 theorem
b. Vector
c. BDDC
d. Linear partial differential operator

15. A surface normal to a flat surface is a vector which is perpendicular to that surface. A normal to a non-flat surface at a point P on the surface is a vector perpendicular to the tangent plane to that surface at P. The word 'normal' is also used as an adjective: a line normal to a plane, the normal component of a force, the _____, etc. The concept of normality generalizes to orthogonality.

a. Normal line
b. Hyperbolic paraboloid
c. Paraboloid
d. Normal vector

16. In mathematics, a (topological) _____ is defined as follows: let I be an interval of real numbers (i.e. a non-empty connected subset of $\mathbb{R}$); then a _____ γ is a continuous mapping $\gamma : I \to X$, where X is a topological space. The _____ γ is said to be simple if it is injective, i.e. if for all x, y in I, we have $\gamma(x) = \gamma(y) \implies x = y$. If I is a closed bounded interval $[a, b]$, we also allow the possibility $\gamma(a) = \gamma(b)$ (this convention makes it possible to talk about closed simple _____.)

a. Curve
b. Closed curve
c. Tractrix
d. Prolate cycloid

17. In mathematics, _____ is one of the basic operations defining a vector space in linear algebra Note that _____ is different from scalar product which is an inner product between two vectors.

More specifically, if K is a field and V is a vector space over K, then _____ is a function from K × V to V. The result of applying this function to c in K and v in V is denoted cv.

a. Direction cosines
b. Vector-valued function
c. Homogeneous function
d. Scalar multiplication

18. In a totally ordered set all elements are mutually comparable, so such a set can have at most one minimal element and at most one maximal element. Then, due to mutual comparability, the minimal element will also be the least element and the maximal element will also be the greatest element. Thus in a totally ordered set we can simply use the terms minimum and _____.

a. Racetrack principle
b. Leibniz rule
c. Maximum
d. Nth term

19. In calculus, the _____ is a formula for the derivative of the composite of two functions.

Chapter 14. DIFFERENTIATING FUNCTIONS OF SEVERAL VARIABLES

In intuitive terms, if a variable, y, depends on a second variable, u, which in turn depends on a third variable, x, then the rate of change of y with respect to x can be computed as the rate of change of y with respect to u multiplied by the rate of change of u with respect to x. Schematically,

$$\frac{dy}{dx} = \frac{dy}{du} \cdot \frac{du}{dx}.$$

a. Differentiation rules
c. Product rule
b. Reciprocal Rule
d. Chain rule

20. In mathematics, a _____ represents the application of one function to the results of another. For instance, the functions f: X → Y and g: Y → Z can be composed by first computing f(x) and then applying a function g to the output of f(x.)

Thus one obtains a function g ∘ f: X → Z defined by (g ∘ f)(x) = g(f(x)) for all x in X. The notation g ∘ f is read as 'g circle f', or 'g composed with f', 'g after f', 'g following f', or just 'g of f'.

a. Surjective
c. Piecewise-defined function
b. Constant function
d. Composite function

21. In mathematics, a _____ is a function with multiplicative scaling behaviour: if the argument is multiplied by a factor, then the result is multiplied by some power of this factor.

Suppose that $f : V \to W$ is a function between two vector spaces over a field F.

We say that f is homogeneous of degree k if

$$f(\alpha \mathbf{v}) = \alpha^k f(\mathbf{v})$$

for all nonzero $\alpha \in F$ and $\mathbf{v} \in V$.

a. Direction vector
c. Dot product
b. Direction cosines
d. Homogeneous function

22. Integration is an important concept in mathematics, specifically in the field of calculus and, more broadly, mathematical analysis. Given a function f of a real variable x and an interval [a, b] of the real line, the _____

$$\int_a^b f(x)\, dx,$$

is defined informally to be the net signed area of the region in the xy-plane bounded by the graph of f, the x-axis, and the vertical lines x = a and x = b.

The term '_____' may also refer to the notion of antiderivative, a function F whose derivative is the given function f.

a. Integral test for convergence
b. Integrand
c. Indefinite integral
d. Integral

23. The _____, L, of a dynamical system is a function that summarizes the dynamics of the system. It is named after Joseph Louis Lagrange. The concept of a _____ was originally introduced in a reformulation of classical mechanics known as _____ mechanics.

a. Vector potential
b. Klein-Gordon equation
c. Dirac equation
d. Lagrangian

24. f'(x) is twice the absolute value function, and it does not have a derivative at zero. Similar examples show that a function can have k derivatives for any non-negative integer k but no (k + 1)-order derivative. A function that has k successive derivatives is called _____.

a. Power series
b. Differential calculus
c. K times differentiable
d. Differential coefficient

Chapter 15. OPTIMIZATION: LOCAL AND GLOBAL EXTREMA

1. In mathematics, a _____ (or critical number) is a point on the domain of a function where:

   - one dimension: the derivative (or slope of the line when visualized) is equal to zero or a point where the function ceases to be differentiable.
   - in general: there are two distinct concepts: either the derivative (Jacobian) vanishes, or it is not of full rank (or, in either case, the function is not differentiable); these agree in one dimension.

   Note that in one dimension, a critical value or critical number x of function f is the domain element at which the derivative is zero or undefined, whereas the associated ordered pair (x, y) is the _____. In higher dimensions a critical value is in the range whereas a _____ is in the domain.

   There are two situations in which a point becomes a _____ of a function of one variable. The first of which is that the value of the first derivative is equal to zero.

   a. Multivariable calculus
   b. Differentiation operator
   c. Total derivative
   d. Critical point

2. In mathematics, a function f defined on some set X with real or complex values is a _____ function, if the set of its values is _____. In other words, there exists a number M>0 such that

   $$|f(x)| \leq M$$

   for all x in X.

   Sometimes, if $f(x) \leq A$ for all x in X, then the function is said to be _____ above by A.

   a. Differential coefficient
   b. Stationary phase approximation
   c. Concave upwards
   d. Bounded

3. A real-valued function f defined on the real line is said to have a _____ point at the point $x^{>*}$, if there exists some $>\varepsilon > 0$, such that $f(x^{>*}) \geq f(x)$ when $|x >- x^{>*}| < >\varepsilon$. The value of the function at this point is called maximum of the function.

   On a graph of a function, its local maxima will look like the tops of hills.

   a. Racetrack principle
   b. Standard part function
   c. Test for Divergence
   d. Local maximum

4. In a totally ordered set all elements are mutually comparable, so such a set can have at most one minimal element and at most one maximal element. Then, due to mutual comparability, the minimal element will also be the least element and the maximal element will also be the greatest element. Thus in a totally ordered set we can simply use the terms minimum and _____.

   a. Maximum
   b. Leibniz rule
   c. Racetrack principle
   d. Nth term

Chapter 15. OPTIMIZATION: LOCAL AND GLOBAL EXTREMA

5. In a totally ordered set all elements are mutually comparable, so such a set can have at most one minimal element and at most one maximal element. Then, due to mutual comparability, the minimal element will also be the least element and the maximal element will also be the greatest element. Thus in a totally ordered set we can simply use the terms _____ and maximum.

    a. Ghosts of departed quantities
    b. Minimum
    c. Nth term
    d. Maximum

6. In economics, the _____ functional form of production functions is widely used to represent the relationship of an output to inputs. It was proposed by Knut Wicksell (1851-1926), and tested against statistical evidence by Charles Cobb and Paul Douglas in 1900-1928.

    For production, the function is

    $$Y = AL^{\alpha}K^{\beta},$$

    where:

    - Y = total production (the monetary value of all goods produced in a year)
    - L = labor input
    - K = capital input
    - A = total factor productivity
    - α and β are the output elasticities of labor and capital, respectively. These values are constants determined by available technology.

    Output elasticity measures the responsiveness of output to a change in levels of either labor or capital used in production, ceteris paribus. For example if α = 0.15, a 1% increase in labor would lead to approximately a 0.15% increase in output.

    a. BDDC
    b. BIBO stability
    c. 15 theorem
    d. Cobb-Douglas

7. In elementary algebra, _____ is a technique for converting a quadratic polynomial of the form

    $$ax^2 + bx + c$$

    to the form

    $$a(\cdots\cdots)^2 + \text{constant}.$$

    The expression inside the parenthesis is of the form x − constant. Thus one converts ax² + bx + c to

    $$a(x - h)^2 + k$$

    and one must find h and k.

_____ is used in

- solving quadratic equations,
- graphing quadratic functions,
- evaluating integrals in calculus,
- finding Laplace transforms.

In mathematics, _____ is considered a basic algebraic operation, and is often applied without remark in any computation involving quadratic polynomials.

There is a simple formula in elementary algebra for computing the square of a binomial:

$$(x+p)^2 = x^2 + 2px + p^2.$$

For example:

$$(x+3)^2 = x^2 + 6x + 9 \quad (p=3)$$
$$(x-5)^2 = x^2 - 10x + 25 \quad (p=-5).$$

In any perfect square, the number p is always half the coefficient of x, and then the constant term is equal to p^2.

a. Hurwitz quaternion order
b. Closed-form expression
c. Multinomial theorem
d. Completing the square

8. The _____, L, of a dynamical system is a function that summarizes the dynamics of the system. It is named after Joseph Louis Lagrange. The concept of a _____ was originally introduced in a reformulation of classical mechanics known as _____ mechanics.

a. Vector potential
b. Dirac equation
c. Lagrangian
d. Klein-Gordon equation

9. Let f be a differentiable function, and let f'(x) be its derivative. The derivative of f'(x) (if it has one) is written f''(x) and is called the _____ of f. Similarly, the derivative of a _____, if it exists, is written f'''(x) and is called the third derivative of f.

a. Stationary phase approximation
b. Vertical asymptote
c. Slant asymptote
d. Second derivative

10. In calculus, a branch of mathematics, the _____ is a criterion often useful for determining whether a given stationary point of a function is a local maximum or a local minimum.

Chapter 15. OPTIMIZATION: LOCAL AND GLOBAL EXTREMA

The test states: If the function f is twice differentiable at a stationary point x, meaning that $f'(x) = 0$, then:

- If $f''(x) < 0$ then f has a local maximum at x.
- If $f''(x) > 0$ then f has a local minimum at x.
- If $f''(x) = 0$, the _____ says nothing about the point x, has a possible inflection point.

In the last case, the function may have a local maximum or minimum there, but the function is sufficiently 'flat' that this is undetected by the second derivative. In this case one has to examine the third derivative. Such an example is f(x) = x⁴.

a. Linearity of differentiation
b. Symmetric derivative
c. Second derivative test
d. Stationary point

11. In calculus, a branch of mathematics, the _____ is a measurement of how a function changes when its input changes. Loosely speaking, a _____ can be thought of as how much a quantity is changing at some given point. For example, the _____ of the position (or distance) of a vehicle with respect to time is the instantaneous velocity (respectively, instantaneous speed) at which the vehicle is traveling.

The process of finding a _____ is called differentiation. The fundamental theorem of calculus states that differentiation is the reverse process to integration.

a. Semi-differentiability
b. Stationary phase approximation
c. Bounded function
d. Derivative

12. In mathematics, a _____ is a point in the domain of a function of two variables which is a stationary point but not a local extremum. At such a point, in general, the surface resembles a saddle that curves up in one direction, and curves down in a different direction (like a mountain pass.) In terms of contour lines, a _____ can be recognized, in general, by a contour that appears to intersect itself.

a. BDDC
b. BIBO stability
c. Saddle point
d. 15 theorem

13. In mathematics, the _____ is the surface defined by the equation

$$z = x^3 - 3xy^2.$$

It belongs to the class of saddle surfaces and its name derives from the observation that a saddle for a monkey requires three depressions: two for the legs, and one for the tail. The point (0,0,0) on the _____ corresponds to a degenerate critical point of the function z(x,y) at (0, 0.) The _____ has an isolated umbilic point with zero Gaussian curvature at the origin, while the curvature is strictly negative at all other points.

Chapter 15. OPTIMIZATION: LOCAL AND GLOBAL EXTREMA

a. Second partial derivatives test
b. Contact
c. Shift theorem
d. Monkey saddle

14. In mathematics, the simplest case of _____ refers to the study of problems in which one seeks to minimize or maximize a real function by systematically choosing the values of real or integer variables from within an allowed set. This (a scalar real valued objective function) is actually a small subset of this field which comprises a large area of applied mathematics and generalizes to study of means to obtain 'best available' values of some objective function given a defined domain where the elaboration is on the types of functions and the conditions and nature of the objects in the problem domain.

The first _____ technique, which is known as steepest descent, goes back to Gauss.

a. ACTRAN
b. Optimization
c. AUSM
d. ALGOR

15. In mathematics, a (topological) _____ is defined as follows: let I be an interval of real numbers (i.e. a non-empty connected subset of $\mathbb{R}$); then a _____ γ is a continuous mapping $\gamma : I \to X$, where X is a topological space. The _____ γ is said to be simple if it is injective, i.e. if for all x, y in I, we have $\gamma(x) = \gamma(y) \implies x = y$. If I is a closed bounded interval $[a, b]$, we also allow the possibility $\gamma(a) = \gamma(b)$ (this convention makes it possible to talk about closed simple _____.)

a. Tractrix
b. Curve
c. Closed curve
d. Prolate cycloid

16. The method of _____ or ordinary _____ is used to solve overdetermined systems. _____ is often applied in statistical contexts, particularly regression analysis.

_____ can be interpreted as a method of fitting data. The best fit in the _____ sense is that instance of the model for which the sum of squared residuals has its least value, a residual being the difference between an observed value and the value given by the model.

a. 15 theorem
b. BDDC
c. BIBO stability
d. Least squares

17. In mathematics, a _____ is a constant multiplicative factor of a certain object. For example, in the expression $9x^2$, the _____ of x^2 is 9.

The object can be such things as a variable, a vector, a function, etc.

a. Resultant
b. Binomial type
c. Degree of the polynomial
d. Coefficient

18. In metric topology and related fields of mathematics, a set U is called _____ if, intuitively speaking, starting from any point x in U one can move by a small amount in any direction and still be in the set U. In other words, the distance between any point x in U and the edge of U is always greater than zero.

Chapter 15. OPTIMIZATION: LOCAL AND GLOBAL EXTREMA

As an example, consider the _____ interval (0, 1) consisting of all real numbers x with 0 < x < 1. Here, the topology is the usual topology on the real line. We can look at this in two ways.

a. AUSM
b. ACTRAN
c. Open
d. ALGOR

19. In mathematics, the interior of a set S consists of all points of S that are intuitively 'not on the edge of S'. A point that is in the interior of S is an _____ of S.

The exterior of a set is the interior of its complement; it consists of the points that are not in the set or its boundary.

a. Interior Point
b. ALGOR
c. ACTRAN
d. AUSM

20. In mathematical optimization, the method of Lagrange multipliers provides a strategy for finding the maximum/minimum of a function subject to constraints.

For example, consider the optimization problem

$$\text{maximize } f(x,y)$$
$$\text{subject to } g(x,y) = c.$$

We introduce a new variable (λ) called a _____, and study the Lagrange function defined by

$$\Lambda(x,y,\lambda) = f(x,y) - \lambda\big(g(x,y) - c\big).$$

If (x,y)≉ is a maximum for the original constrained problem, then there exists a λ such that (x,y,λ)≉ is a stationary point for the Lagrange function (stationary points are those points where the partial derivatives of Λ are zero.) However, not all stationary points yield a solution of the original problem.

a. BDDC
b. BIBO stability
c. 15 theorem
d. Lagrange multiplier

21. In mathematics, a _____ decomposes a periodic function into a sum of simple oscillating functions, namely sines and cosines (or complex exponentials.) The study of _____ is a branch of Fourier analysis. _____ were introduced by Joseph Fourier (1768-1830) for the purpose of solving the heat equation in a metal plate.

a. BDDC
b. 15 theorem
c. BIBO stability
d. Fourier series

Chapter 16. INTEGRATING FUNCTIONS OF SEVERAL VARIABLES

1. Integration is an important concept in mathematics, specifically in the field of calculus and, more broadly, mathematical analysis. Given a function f of a real variable x and an interval [a, b] of the real line, the _____

$$\int_a^b f(x)\, dx,$$

is defined informally to be the net signed area of the region in the xy-plane bounded by the graph of f, the x-axis, and the vertical lines x = a and x = b.

The term '_____' may also refer to the notion of antiderivative, a function F whose derivative is the given function f.

   a. Integral test for convergence   b. Integral
   c. Indefinite integral   d. Integrand

2. The _____ of a material is defined as its mass per unit volume. The symbol of _____ is ρ '>rho.)

Mathematically:

$$d = \frac{m}{V}$$

where:

        d is the _____,
        m is the mass,
        V is the volume.

   a. BDDC   b. 15 theorem
   c. BIBO stability   d. Density

3. The _____ specifies the relationship between the two central operations of calculus, differentiation and integration.

The first part of the theorem, sometimes called the first _____, shows that an indefinite integration can be reversed by a differentiation.

The second part, sometimes called the second _____, allows one to compute the definite integral of a function by using any one of its infinitely many antiderivatives.

   a. Leibniz formula   b. Limits of integration
   c. Periodic function   d. Fundamental Theorem of Calculus

4. In mathematics, a _____ is a method for approximating the total area underneath a curve on a graph, otherwise known as an integral. It may also be used to define the integration operation.

Chapter 16. INTEGRATING FUNCTIONS OF SEVERAL VARIABLES

Consider a function $f: D \rightarrow \mathbf{R}$, where D is a subset of the real numbers $\mathbf{R}$, and let $I = [a, b]$ be a closed interval contained in D. A finite set of points $\{x_0, x_1, x_2, \ldots x_n\}$ such that $a = x_0 < x_1 < x_2 \ldots < x_n = b$ creates a partition

$$P = \{[x_0, x_1], [x_1, x_2], \ldots [x_{n-1}, x_n]\}$$

of I.

- a. Signed measure
- b. Solid of revolution
- c. Risch algorithm
- d. Riemann sum

5. In mathematics and its applications, a _____ system is a system for assigning an n-tuple of numbers or scalars to each point in an n-dimensional space. This concept is part of the theory of manifolds. 'Scalars' in many cases means real numbers, but, depending on context, can mean complex numbers or elements of some other commutative ring.
- a. Cylindrical coordinate system
- b. 15 theorem
- c. Spherical coordinate system
- d. Coordinate

6. In acoustics and telecommunication, a _____ of a wave is a component frequency of the signal that is an integer multiple of the fundamental frequency. For example, if the fundamental frequency is f, the harmonics have frequencies f, 2f, 3f, 4f, etc. The harmonics have the property that they are all periodic at the fundamental frequency, therefore the sum of harmonics is also periodic at that frequency.
- a. 15 theorem
- b. BDDC
- c. BIBO stability
- d. Harmonic

7. In mathematics, the _____ is the infinite series

$$\sum_{k=1}^{\infty} \frac{1}{k} = 1 + \frac{1}{2} + \frac{1}{3} + \frac{1}{4} + \cdots.$$

Its name derives from the concept of overtones, or harmonics, in music: the wavelengths of the overtones of a vibrating string are 1/2, 1/3, 1/4, etc., of the string's fundamental wavelength. Every term of the series after the first is the harmonic mean of the neighboring terms; the term harmonic mean likewise derives from music.

The _____ diverges to infinity, albeit rather slowly (the first 10^{43} terms sum to less than 100 .)

- a. 15 theorem
- b. BDDC
- c. BIBO stability
- d. Harmonic series

8. Just as the definite integral of a positive function of one variable represents the area of the region between the graph of the function and the x-axis, the _____ of a positive function of two variables represents the volume of the region between the surface defined by the function (on the three dimensional Cartesian plane where z = f(x,y)) and the plane which contains its domain. (Note that the same volume can be obtained via the triple integral -- the integral of a function in three variables -- of the constant function f(x, y, z) = 1 over the above-mentioned region between the surface and the plane.) If there are more variables, a multiple integral will yield hypervolumes of multi-dimensional functions.

Chapter 16. INTEGRATING FUNCTIONS OF SEVERAL VARIABLES

a. Double integral
b. Risch algorithm
c. Trigonometric substitution
d. Constant of integration

9. In mathematics, the concept of a '_____' is used to describe the behavior of a function as its argument or input either 'gets close' to some point, or as the argument becomes arbitrarily large; or the behavior of a sequence's elements as their index increases indefinitely. Limits are used in calculus and other branches of mathematical analysis to define derivatives and continuity.

In formulas, _____ is usually abbreviated as lim

a. Limit
b. BIBO stability
c. 15 theorem
d. BDDC

10. In mathematics, the _____ is a two-dimensional coordinate system in which each point on a plane is determined by an angle and a distance. The _____ is especially useful in situations where the relationship between two points is most easily expressed in terms of angles and distance; in the more familiar Cartesian or rectangular coordinate system, such a relationship can only be found through trigonometric formulation.

As the coordinate system is two-dimensional, each point is determined by two polar coordinates: the radial coordinate and the angular coordinate.

a. BDDC
b. Polar coordinate system
c. BIBO stability
d. 15 theorem

11. The concept of _____ in mathematics evolved from the concept of _____ in physics. The nth _____ of a real-valued function f(x) of a real variable about a value c is

$$\mu'_n = \int_{-\infty}^{\infty} (x-c)^n f(x)\,dx.$$

It is possible to define moments for random variables in a more general fashion than moments for real values. See Moments in metric spaces.

a. Geometric mean
b. Median
c. Poisson distribution
d. Moment

12. A _____ is one of the most curvilinear basic geometric shapes:It has two faces, zero vertices, and zero edges. The surface formed by the points at a fixed distance from a given straight line, the axis of the _____. The solid enclosed by this surface and by two planes perpendicular to the axis is also called a _____.

a. 15 theorem
b. Right circular cylinder
c. BDDC
d. Cylinder

13. In mathematics, a _____ provides a means for integrating a function with respect to volume in various coordinate systems such as spherical coordinates and cylindrical coordinates. More generally, a _____ is a measure on a manifold.

Chapter 16. INTEGRATING FUNCTIONS OF SEVERAL VARIABLES

On an orientable n-manifold, the _____ typically arises from a volume form: a differential form of degree n which is nowhere equal to zero.

a. BDDC
c. 15 theorem
b. Volume element
d. BIBO stability

14. In economics, the _____ functional form of production functions is widely used to represent the relationship of an output to inputs. It was proposed by Knut Wicksell (1851-1926), and tested against statistical evidence by Charles Cobb and Paul Douglas in 1900-1928.

For production, the function is

$$Y = AL^{\alpha}K^{\beta},$$

where:

- Y = total production (the monetary value of all goods produced in a year)
- L = labor input
- K = capital input
- A = total factor productivity
- α and β are the output elasticities of labor and capital, respectively. These values are constants determined by available technology.

Output elasticity measures the responsiveness of output to a change in levels of either labor or capital used in production, ceteris paribus. For example if α = 0.15, a 1% increase in labor would lead to approximately a 0.15% increase in output.

a. BDDC
c. BIBO stability
b. 15 theorem
d. Cobb-Douglas

15. In vector calculus, the _____ is shorthand for either the _____ matrix or its determinant, the _____ determinant.

In algebraic geometry the _____ of a curve means the _____ variety: a group variety associated to the curve, in which the curve can be embedded.

These concepts are all named after the mathematician Carl Gustav Jacob Jacobi.

a. Critical point
c. Saddle surface
b. Vector Laplacian
d. Jacobian

16. In mathematics, a _____ is a basic technique used to simplify problems in which the original variables are replaced with new ones; the new and old variables being related in some specified way. The intent is that the problem expressed in new variables may be simpler, or else equivalent to a better understood problem.

Chapter 16. INTEGRATING FUNCTIONS OF SEVERAL VARIABLES

A very simple example of a useful variable change can be seen in the problem of finding the roots of the eighth order polynomial:

$$x^8 + 3x^4 + 2 = 0$$

Eighth order polynomial equations are generally impossible to solve in terms of elementary functions.

a. Linear equation
c. Cubic function
b. Change of variables
d. Quadratic formula

Chapter 17. PARAMETERIZATION AND VECTOR FIELDS

1. In mathematics, a (topological) _____ is defined as follows: let I be an interval of real numbers (i.e. a non-empty connected subset of $\mathbb{R}$); then a _____ γ is a continuous mapping $\gamma : I \to X$, where X is a topological space. The _____ γ is said to be simple if it is injective, i.e. if for all x, y in I, we have $\gamma(x) = \gamma(y) \implies x = y$. If I is a closed bounded interval $[a, b]$, we also allow the possibility $\gamma(a) = \gamma(b)$ (this convention makes it possible to talk about closed simple _____.)
   - a. Closed curve
   - b. Tractrix
   - c. Prolate cycloid
   - d. Curve

2. A _____ is a special kind of space curve, i.e. a smooth curve in three-space. As a mental image of a _____ one may take the spring (although the spring is not a curve, and so is technically not a _____, it does give a convenient mental picture.) A _____ is characterised by the fact that the tangent line at any point makes a constant angle with a fixed line.
   - a. 15 theorem
   - b. BDDC
   - c. BIBO stability
   - d. Helix

3. In mathematics, _____ are a method of defining a curve. A simple kinematical example is when one uses a time parameter to determine the position, velocity, and other information about a body in motion.

   Abstractly, a relation is given in the form of an equation, and it is shown also to be the image of functions from items such as R^n.
   - a. Critical point
   - b. Shift theorem
   - c. Partial derivative
   - d. Parametric equations

4. In elementary mathematics, physics, and engineering, a _____ is a geometric object that has both a magnitude (or length), direction and sense, (i.e., orientation along the given direction.) A _____ is frequently represented by a line segment with a definite direction, or graphically as an arrow, connecting an initial point A with a terminal point B, and denoted by

   The magnitude of the _____ is the length of the segment and the direction characterizes the displacement of B relative to A: how much one should move the point A to 'carry' it to the point B.

   Many algebraic operations on real numbers have close analogues for vectors.
   - a. 15 theorem
   - b. Linear partial differential operator
   - c. BDDC
   - d. Vector

5. In physics, _____ is defined as the rate of change of position. it is vector physical quantity; both speed and direction are required to define it. In the SI (metric) system, it is measured in meters per second: (m/s) or ms^{-1}.
   - a. BIBO stability
   - b. BDDC
   - c. 15 theorem
   - d. Velocity

Chapter 17. PARAMETERIZATION AND VECTOR FIELDS

6. In geometry, the _____ (or simply the tangent) to a curve at a given point is the straight line that 'just touches' the curve at that point (in the sense explained more precisely below.) As it passes through the point of tangency, the _____ is 'going in the same direction' as the curve, and in this sense it is the best straight-line approximation to the curve at that point. The same definition applies to space curves and curves in n-dimensional Euclidean space.
    a. Tangent line
    b. Lie derivative
    c. North pole
    d. Minimal surface

7. In physics, and more specifically kinematics, _____ is the change in velocity over time. Because velocity is a vector, it can change in two ways: a change in magnitude and/or a change in direction. In one dimension, _____ is the rate at which something speeds up or slows down.
    a. Acceleration
    b. ALGOR
    c. ACTRAN
    d. AUSM

8. In mathematics, the hyperbolic functions are analogs of the ordinary trigonometric functions. The basic hyperbolic functions are the hyperbolic sine 'sinh', and the _____ 'cosh', from which are derived the hyperbolic tangent 'tanh', etc., in analogy to the derived trigonometric functions. The inverse hyperbolic functions are the area hyperbolic sine 'arsinh' (also called 'asinh', or sometimes by the misnomer of 'arcsinh') and so on.
    a. Square root function
    b. Hyperbolic tangent
    c. Step function
    d. Hyperbolic cosine

9. In mathematics, the concept of a '_____' is used to describe the behavior of a function as its argument or input either 'gets close' to some point, or as the argument becomes arbitrarily large; or the behavior of a sequence's elements as their index increases indefinitely. Limits are used in calculus and other branches of mathematical analysis to define derivatives and continuity.

    In formulas, _____ is usually abbreviated as lim

    a. Limit
    b. BIBO stability
    c. BDDC
    d. 15 theorem

10. _____ is the long dimension of any object. The _____ of a thing is the distance between its ends, its linear extent as measured from end to end. This may be distinguished from height, which is vertical extent, and width or breadth, which are the distance from side to side, measuring across the object at right angles to the _____.
    a. BDDC
    b. Length
    c. 15 theorem
    d. BIBO stability

11. In mathematics a _____ is a construction in vector calculus which associates a vector to every point in a (locally) Euclidean space.

Vector fields are often used in physics to model, for example, the speed and direction of a moving fluid throughout space, or the strength and direction of some force, such as the magnetic or gravitational force, as it changes from point to point.

In the rigorous mathematical treatment, (tangent) vector fields are defined on manifolds as sections of a manifold's tangent bundle.

a. BDDC
b. BIBO stability
c. 15 theorem
d. Vector field

12. A _____ is a model used within physics to explain how gravity exists in the universe. In its original concept, gravity was a force between point masses. Following Newton, Laplace attempted to model gravity as some kind of radiation field or fluid, and since the 19th century explanations for gravity have usually been sought in terms of a field model, rather than a point attraction.

a. 15 theorem
b. BDDC
c. BIBO stability
d. Gravitational field

13. A _____, sometimes known as an energy shield, force shield typically made of energy or charged particles, that protects a person, area or object from attacks or intrusions.

A University of Washington in Seattle group has been experimenting with using a bubble of charged plasma to surround a spacecraft, contained by a fine mesh of superconducting wire. This would protect the spacecraft from interstellar radiation and some particles without needing physical shielding.

a. 15 theorem
b. BDDC
c. BIBO stability
d. Force Field

14. In vector calculus, the _____ of a scalar field is a vector field which points in the direction of the greatest rate of increase of the scalar field, and whose magnitude is the greatest rate of change.

A generalization of the _____ for functions on a Euclidean space which have values in another Euclidean space is the Jacobian. A further generalization for a function from one Banach space to another is the Fréchet derivative.

a. Symmetric derivative
b. Smooth function
c. Lin-Tsien equation
d. Gradient

15. Integration is an important concept in mathematics, specifically in the field of calculus and, more broadly, mathematical analysis. Given a function f of a real variable x and an interval [a, b] of the real line, the _____

$$\int_a^b f(x)\,dx,$$

is defined informally to be the net signed area of the region in the xy-plane bounded by the graph of f, the x-axis, and the vertical lines x = a and x = b.

The term '_____' may also refer to the notion of antiderivative, a function F whose derivative is the given function f.

a. Integral test for convergence
b. Indefinite integral
c. Integral
d. Integrand

Chapter 17. PARAMETERIZATION AND VECTOR FIELDS

16. In mathematics, an _____ is a parametric curve that represents a specific solution to an ordinary differential equation or system of equations. If the differential equation is represented as a vector field or slope field, then the corresponding integral curves are tangent to the field at each point.

Integral curves are known by various other names, depending on the nature and interpretation of the differential equation or vector field.

- a. Unit tangent vector
- b. Invariant differential operator
- c. ACTRAN
- d. Integral Curve

17. A _____ is one of the most curvilinear basic geometric shapes:It has two faces, zero vertices, and zero edges. The surface formed by the points at a fixed distance from a given straight line, the axis of the _____. The solid enclosed by this surface and by two planes perpendicular to the axis is also called a _____.
- a. Right circular cylinder
- b. BDDC
- c. Cylinder
- d. 15 theorem

18. A _____ is a surface created by rotating a curve lying on some plane (the generatrix) around a straight line (the axis of rotation) that lies on the same plane.

Examples of surfaces generated by a straight line are the cylindrical and conical surfaces. A circle that is rotated about a (coplanar) axis through the center generates a sphere.

- a. Constant of integration
- b. Riemann sum
- c. Shell integration
- d. Surface of revolution

19. A _____ is perfectly round geometrical object in three-dimensional space, such as the shape of a round ball. Like a circle in two dimensions, a perfect _____ is completely symmetrical around its center, with all points on the surface lying the same distance r from the center point. This distance r is known as the radius of the _____.
- a. Minimal surface
- b. Sphere
- c. North pole
- d. Tangent line

20. In mathematics and its applications, a _____ system is a system for assigning an n-tuple of numbers or scalars to each point in an n-dimensional space. This concept is part of the theory of manifolds. 'Scalars' in many cases means real numbers, but, depending on context, can mean complex numbers or elements of some other commutative ring.
- a. 15 theorem
- b. Coordinate
- c. Spherical coordinate system
- d. Cylindrical coordinate system

21. In geometry, the _____ is a particular mapping (function) that projects a sphere onto a plane. The projection is defined on the entire sphere, except at one point -- the projection point. Where it is defined, the mapping is smooth and bijective.
- a. Peirce quincuncial projection
- b. BDDC
- c. 15 theorem
- d. Stereographic projection

Chapter 18. LINE INTEGRALS

1. In mathematics, a _____ is an integral where the function to be integrated is evaluated along a curve. Various different line integrals are in use. A specific case of an integration along a closed curve in two dimensions or the complex plane is the contour integral.
   - a. Radius of convergence
   - b. Picard theorem
   - c. Mittag-Leffler star
   - d. Line integral

2. In mathematics, an _____ on a real vector space is a choice of which ordered bases are 'positively' oriented and which are 'negatively' oriented. In the three-dimensional Euclidean space, the two possible basis orientations are called right-handed and left-handed (or right-chiral and left-chiral), respectively. However, the choice of _____ is independent of the handedness or chirality of the bases (although right-handed bases are typically declared to be positively oriented, they may also be assigned a negative _____.)
   - a. Orientation
   - b. Unit vector
   - c. ALGOR
   - d. ACTRAN

3. In mathematics, a (topological) _____ is defined as follows: let I be an interval of real numbers (i.e. a non-empty connected subset of $\mathbb{R}$); then a _____ γ is a continuous mapping $\gamma : I \to X$, where X is a topological space. The _____ γ is said to be simple if it is injective, i.e. if for all x, y in I, we have $\gamma(x) = \gamma(y) \implies x = y$. If I is a closed bounded interval $[a, b]$, we also allow the possibility $\gamma(a) = \gamma(b)$ (this convention makes it possible to talk about closed simple _____.)
   - a. Prolate cycloid
   - b. Closed curve
   - c. Tractrix
   - d. Curve

4. Integration is an important concept in mathematics, specifically in the field of calculus and, more broadly, mathematical analysis. Given a function f of a real variable x and an interval [a, b] of the real line, the _____

$$\int_a^b f(x)\,dx,$$

is defined informally to be the net signed area of the region in the xy-plane bounded by the graph of f, the x-axis, and the vertical lines x = a and x = b.

The term '_____' may also refer to the notion of antiderivative, a function F whose derivative is the given function f.

   - a. Integral test for convergence
   - b. Integral
   - c. Indefinite integral
   - d. Integrand

5. The _____ specifies the relationship between the two central operations of calculus, differentiation and integration.

The first part of the theorem, sometimes called the first _____, shows that an indefinite integration can be reversed by a differentiation.

The second part, sometimes called the second _____, allows one to compute the definite integral of a function by using any one of its infinitely many antiderivatives.

a. Periodic function
b. Fundamental Theorem of Calculus
c. Limits of integration
d. Leibniz formula

6. In mathematics, a _____ is a function whose definition is dependent on the value of the independent variable. Mathematically, a real-valued function f of a real variable x is a relationship whose definition is given differently on disjoint subsets of its domain

The word piecewise is also used to describe any property of a _____ that holds for each piece but may not hold for the whole domain of the function.

a. Constant function
b. Surjective
c. Range
d. Piecewise-defined function

7. In elementary mathematics, physics, and engineering, a _____ is a geometric object that has both a magnitude (or length), direction and sense, (i.e., orientation along the given direction.) A _____ is frequently represented by a line segment with a definite direction, or graphically as an arrow, connecting an initial point A with a terminal point B, and denoted by

The magnitude of the _____ is the length of the segment and the direction characterizes the displacement of B relative to A: how much one should move the point A to 'carry' it to the point B.

Many algebraic operations on real numbers have close analogues for vectors.

a. 15 theorem
b. BDDC
c. Linear partial differential operator
d. Vector

8. In mathematics a _____ is a construction in vector calculus which associates a vector to every point in a (locally) Euclidean space.

Vector fields are often used in physics to model, for example, the speed and direction of a moving fluid throughout space, or the strength and direction of some force, such as the magnetic or gravitational force, as it changes from point to point.

In the rigorous mathematical treatment, (tangent) vector fields are defined on manifolds as sections of a manifold's tangent bundle.

a. 15 theorem
b. Vector field
c. BIBO stability
d. BDDC

9. A _____ is a type of manifold that is locally similar enough to Euclidean space to allow one to do calculus Any manifold can be described by a collection of charts, also known as an atlas.

Chapter 18. LINE INTEGRALS

a. Tangent line
b. Minimal surface
c. Sphere
d. Differentiable manifold

10. In mathematics, _____ is one of the basic operations defining a vector space in linear algebra Note that _____ is different from scalar product which is an inner product between two vectors.

More specifically, if K is a field and V is a vector space over K, then _____ is a function from K × V to V. The result of applying this function to c in K and v in V is denoted cv.

a. Direction cosines
b. Vector-valued function
c. Homogeneous function
d. Scalar multiplication

11. _____ or isopotential in mathematics and physics (especially electronics) refers to a region in space where every point in it is at the same potential. This usually refers to a scalar potential, although it can also be applied to vector potentials. Often, _____ surfaces are used to visualize an (n)-dimensional scalar potential function in (n-1) dimensional space.

a. Equipotential
b. Upper convected time derivative
c. Implicit function theorem
d. Inverse function theorem

12. In vector calculus, the _____ of a scalar field is a vector field which points in the direction of the greatest rate of increase of the scalar field, and whose magnitude is the greatest rate of change.

A generalization of the _____ for functions on a Euclidean space which have values in another Euclidean space is the Jacobian. A further generalization for a function from one Banach space to another is the Fréchet derivative.

a. Symmetric derivative
b. Lin-Tsien equation
c. Smooth function
d. Gradient

13. _____ is the practice of decreasing the quantity of energy used. It may be achieved through efficient energy use, in which case energy use is decreased while achieving a similar outcome, or by reduced consumption of energy services.
_____ may result in increase of financial capital, environmental value, national security, personal security, and human comfort.

a. AUSM
b. Energy conservation
c. ALGOR
d. ACTRAN

14. A vector field V defined on a set S is called a _____ or a conservative field if there exists a real valued function (a scalar field) f on S such that

$$V = \nabla f.$$

The associated flow is called the gradient flow, and is used in the method of gradient descent.

The path integral along any closed curve γ (γ(0) = γ(1)) in a _____ is zero:

$$\int_\gamma \langle V(x), dx \rangle = \int_\gamma \langle \nabla f(x), dx \rangle = f(\gamma(1)) - f(\gamma(0))$$

a. BDDC
c. BIBO stability
b. 15 theorem
d. Gradient field

15. _____ can be thought of as energy stored within a physical system. It is called _____ because it has the potential to be converted into other forms of energy, such as kinetic energy, and to do work in the process. The standard (SI) unit of measure for _____ is the joule, the same as for work or energy in general.
   a. Potential Energy
   b. Law of Conservation of Energy
   c. BDDC
   d. 15 theorem

16. The _____, L, of a dynamical system is a function that summarizes the dynamics of the system. It is named after Joseph Louis Lagrange. The concept of a _____ was originally introduced in a reformulation of classical mechanics known as _____ mechanics.
   a. Klein-Gordon equation
   b. Lagrangian
   c. Dirac equation
   d. Vector potential

17. In mathematics and its applications, a _____ system is a system for assigning an n-tuple of numbers or scalars to each point in an n-dimensional space. This concept is part of the theory of manifolds. 'Scalars' in many cases means real numbers, but, depending on context, can mean complex numbers or elements of some other commutative ring.
   a. Cylindrical coordinate system
   b. 15 theorem
   c. Coordinate
   d. Spherical coordinate system

Chapter 19. FLUX INTEGRALS

1. In vector calculus, the _____ is an operator that measures the magnitude of a vector field's source or sink at a given point; the _____ of a vector field is a (signed) scalar. For example, consider air as it is heated or cooled. The relevant vector field for this example is the velocity of the moving air at a point.
   - a. Green's theorem
   - b. Triple product
   - c. Gradient theorem
   - d. Divergence

2. In vector calculus, the _____ Ostrogradskye;s theorem the _____ states that the outward flux of a vector field through a surface is equal to the triple integral of the divergence on the region inside the surface. Intuitively, it states that the sum of all sources minus the sum of all sinks gives the net flow out of a region.
   - a. Divergence
   - b. Divergence Theorem
   - c. Del
   - d. Green's theorem

3. In the various subfields of physics, there exist two common usages of the term _____, both with rigorous mathematical frameworks.

   - In the study of transport phenomena (heat transfer, mass transfer and fluid dynamics), _____ is defined as the amount that flows through a unit area per unit time. _____ in this definition is a vector.
   - In the field of electromagnetism and mathematics, _____ is usually the integral of a vector quantity over a finite surface. The result of this integration is a scalar quantity. The magnetic _____ is thus the integral of the magnetic vector field B over a surface, and the electric _____ is defined similarly. Using this definition, the _____ of the Poynting vector over a specified surface is the rate at which electromagnetic energy flows through that surface. Confusingly, the Poynting vector is sometimes called the power _____, which is an example of the first usage of _____, above. It has units of watts per square metre (WÂ·m^{-2})

   One could argue, based on the work of James Clerk Maxwell, that the transport definition precedes the more recent way the term is used in electromagnetism. The specific quote from Maxwell is 'In the case of fluxes, we have to take the integral, over a surface, of the _____ through every element of the surface. The result of this operation is called the surface integral of the _____.

   - a. BIBO stability
   - b. 15 theorem
   - c. Flux
   - d. BDDC

4. In mathematics, an _____ on a real vector space is a choice of which ordered bases are 'positively' oriented and which are 'negatively' oriented. In the three-dimensional Euclidean space, the two possible basis orientations are called right-handed and left-handed (or right-chiral and left-chiral), respectively. However, the choice of _____ is independent of the handedness or chirality of the bases (although right-handed bases are typically declared to be positively oriented, they may also be assigned a negative _____.)
   - a. ALGOR
   - b. Orientation
   - c. Unit vector
   - d. ACTRAN

5. A _____ is a surface created by rotating a curve lying on some plane (the generatrix) around a straight line (the axis of rotation) that lies on the same plane.

Examples of surfaces generated by a straight line are the cylindrical and conical surfaces. A circle that is rotated about a (coplanar) axis through the center generates a sphere.

Chapter 19. FLUX INTEGRALS

a. Shell integration
b. Constant of integration
c. Riemann sum
d. Surface of revolution

6. In elementary mathematics, physics, and engineering, a _____ is a geometric object that has both a magnitude (or length), direction and sense, (i.e., orientation along the given direction.) A _____ is frequently represented by a line segment with a definite direction, or graphically as an arrow, connecting an initial point A with a terminal point B, and denoted by

$$\boxed{}\!\!>$$

The magnitude of the _____ is the length of the segment and the direction characterizes the displacement of B relative to A: how much one should move the point A to 'carry' it to the point B.

Many algebraic operations on real numbers have close analogues for vectors.

a. 15 theorem
b. BDDC
c. Linear partial differential operator
d. Vector

7. In geometry, for a finite planar surface of scalar area S, the _____

$$\mathbf{S}$$

is defined as a vector whose magnitude is S and whose direction is perpendicular to the plane, as determined by the right hand rule on the rim (moving one's right hand counterclockwise around the rim, when the palm of the hand is 'touching' the surface, and the straight thumb indicate the direction.)

$$\mathbf{S} = \hat{\mathbf{n}} S$$

This can only be defined for flat surfaces, or for regions of curved surfaces which are sufficiently small that they can be considered flat.

The concept of an area vector simplifies the equation for determining the flux through the surface.

a. Lipschitz domain
b. Surface area
c. Gyroid
d. Vector area

8. In geometry, for a finite planar surface of scalar area S, the vector area

$$\mathbf{S}$$

is defined as a vector whose magnitude is S and whose direction is perpendicular to the plane, as determined by the right hand rule on the rim (moving one's right hand counterclockwise around the rim, when the palm of the hand is 'touching' the surface, and the straight thumb indicate the direction.)

$$\mathbf{S} = \hat{\mathbf{n}} S$$

This can only be defined for flat surfaces, or for regions of curved surfaces which are sufficiently small that they can be considered flat.

The concept of an _____ simplifies the equation for determining the flux through the surface.

a. Area Vector
b. Orthogonal trajectories
c. ALGOR
d. ACTRAN

9. In mathematics, a (topological) _____ is defined as follows: let I be an interval of real numbers (i.e. a non-empty connected subset of $\mathbb{R}$); then a _____ γ is a continuous mapping $\gamma : I \to X$, where X is a topological space. The _____ γ is said to be simple if it is injective, i.e. if for all x, y in I, we have $\gamma(x) = \gamma(y) \implies x = y$. If I is a closed bounded interval $[a, b]$, we also allow the possibility $\gamma(a) = \gamma(b)$ (this convention makes it possible to talk about closed simple _____.)

a. Prolate cycloid
b. Closed curve
c. Tractrix
d. Curve

10. Integration is an important concept in mathematics, specifically in the field of calculus and, more broadly, mathematical analysis. Given a function f of a real variable x and an interval [a, b] of the real line, the _____

$$\int_a^b f(x)\,dx,$$

is defined informally to be the net signed area of the region in the xy-plane bounded by the graph of f, the x-axis, and the vertical lines x = a and x = b.

The term '_____' may also refer to the notion of antiderivative, a function F whose derivative is the given function f.

a. Integral test for convergence
b. Indefinite integral
c. Integrand
d. Integral

Chapter 20. CALCULUS OF VECTOR FIELDS

1. In mathematics a _____ is a construction in vector calculus which associates a vector to every point in a (locally) Euclidean space.

Vector fields are often used in physics to model, for example, the speed and direction of a moving fluid throughout space, or the strength and direction of some force, such as the magnetic or gravitational force, as it changes from point to point.

In the rigorous mathematical treatment, (tangent) vector fields are defined on manifolds as sections of a manifold's tangent bundle.

   a. BDDC
   b. BIBO stability
   c. Vector field
   d. 15 theorem

2. In mathematics and its applications, a _____ system is a system for assigning an n-tuple of numbers or scalars to each point in an n-dimensional space. This concept is part of the theory of manifolds. 'Scalars' in many cases means real numbers, but, depending on context, can mean complex numbers or elements of some other commutative ring.
   a. Cylindrical coordinate system
   b. 15 theorem
   c. Spherical coordinate system
   d. Coordinate

3. In vector calculus, the _____ is an operator that measures the magnitude of a vector field's source or sink at a given point; the _____ of a vector field is a (signed) scalar. For example, consider air as it is heated or cooled. The relevant vector field for this example is the velocity of the moving air at a point.
   a. Triple product
   b. Gradient theorem
   c. Green's theorem
   d. Divergence

4. In vector calculus a _____ vector field (also known as an incompressible vector field) is a vector field v with divergence zero:

$$\nabla \cdot \mathbf{v} = 0.$$

The fundamental theorem of vector calculus states that any vector field can be expressed as the sum of a conservative vector field and a _____ field. The condition of zero divergence is satisfied whenever a vector field v has only a vector potential component, because the definition of the vector potential A as:

$$\mathbf{v} = \nabla \times \mathbf{A}$$

automatically results in the identity (as can be shown, for example, using Cartesian coordinates):

$$\nabla \cdot \mathbf{v} = \nabla \cdot (\nabla \times \mathbf{A}) = 0.$$

The converse also holds: for any _____ v there exists a vector potential A such that $\mathbf{v} = \nabla \times \mathbf{A}$.

Chapter 20. CALCULUS OF VECTOR FIELDS

The divergence theorem, gives the equivalent integral definition of a _____ field; namely that for any closed surface S, the net total flux through the surface must be zero:

$$\iint_S \mathbf{v} \cdot d\mathbf{s} = 0$$

where $d\mathbf{s}$ is the outward normal to each surface element.

a. Principal part
b. Trigonometric series
c. Bloch space
d. Solenoidal

5. In vector calculus a _____ is a vector field v with divergence zero:

$$\nabla \cdot \mathbf{v} = 0.$$

The fundamental theorem of vector calculus states that any vector field can be expressed as the sum of a conservative vector field and a solenoidal field. The condition of zero divergence is satisfied whenever a vector field v has only a vector potential component, because the definition of the vector potential A as:

$$\mathbf{v} = \nabla \times \mathbf{A}$$

automatically results in the identity (as can be shown, for example, using Cartesian coordinates):

$$\nabla \cdot \mathbf{v} = \nabla \cdot (\nabla \times \mathbf{A}) = 0.$$

The converse also holds: for any solenoidal v there exists a vector potential A such that $\mathbf{v} = \nabla \times \mathbf{A}$.

The divergence theorem, gives the equivalent integral definition of a solenoidal field; namely that for any closed surface S, the net total flux through the surface must be zero:

$$\iint_S \mathbf{v} \cdot d\mathbf{s} = 0$$

where $d\mathbf{s}$ is the outward normal to each surface element.

a. Critical value
b. Principal part
c. Dickman-de Bruijn function
d. Solenoidal vector field

Chapter 20. CALCULUS OF VECTOR FIELDS

6. In elementary mathematics, physics, and engineering, a _____ is a geometric object that has both a magnitude (or length), direction and sense, (i.e., orientation along the given direction.) A _____ is frequently represented by a line segment with a definite direction, or graphically as an arrow, connecting an initial point A with a terminal point B, and denoted by

The magnitude of the _____ is the length of the segment and the direction characterizes the displacement of B relative to A: how much one should move the point A to 'carry' it to the point B.

Many algebraic operations on real numbers have close analogues for vectors.

- a. Vector
- b. 15 theorem
- c. BDDC
- d. Linear partial differential operator

7. In vector calculus, the _____ Ostrogradskye;s theorem the _____ states that the outward flux of a vector field through a surface is equal to the triple integral of the divergence on the region inside the surface. Intuitively, it states that the sum of all sources minus the sum of all sinks gives the net flow out of a region.
- a. Green's theorem
- b. Del
- c. Divergence Theorem
- d. Divergence

8. A _____ is a surface created by rotating a curve lying on some plane (the generatrix) around a straight line (the axis of rotation) that lies on the same plane.

Examples of surfaces generated by a straight line are the cylindrical and conical surfaces. A circle that is rotated about a (coplanar) axis through the center generates a sphere.

- a. Constant of integration
- b. Riemann sum
- c. Shell integration
- d. Surface of revolution

9. A _____ is a model used within physics to explain how gravity exists in the universe. In its original concept, gravity was a force between point masses. Following Newton, Laplace attempted to model gravity as some kind of radiation field or fluid, and since the 19th century explanations for gravity have usually been sought in terms of a field model, rather than a point attraction.
- a. BIBO stability
- b. 15 theorem
- c. Gravitational Field
- d. BDDC

10. In mathematics and physics, the _____ is a common mnemonic for understanding notation conventions for vectors in 3 dimensions. It was invented for use in electromagnetism by British physicist Zachariah William Cole in the late 1800s.

When choosing three vectors that must be at right angles to each other, there are two distinct solutions, so when expressing this idea in mathematics, one must remove the ambiguity of which solution is meant.

Chapter 20. CALCULUS OF VECTOR FIELDS

a. Right-hand rule
c. BIBO stability

b. 15 theorem
d. BDDC

11. The _____ of a material is defined as its mass per unit volume. The symbol of _____ is ρ '>rho.)

Mathematically:

$$d = \frac{m}{V}$$

where:

    d is the _____,
    m is the mass,
    V is the volume.

a. BIBO stability
c. 15 theorem

b. Density
d. BDDC

12. In vector calculus a conservative vector field is a vector field which is the gradient of a scalar potential. There are two closely related concepts: path independence and _____ vector fields. Every conservative vector field has zero curl (and is thus _____), and every conservative vector field has the path independence property.

a. AUSM
c. ACTRAN

b. ALGOR
d. Irrotational

13. In vector calculus, a _____ is a vector field whose curl is a given vector field. This is analogous to a scalar potential, which is a scalar field whose negative gradient is a given vector field.

Formally, given a vector field v, a _____ is a vector field A such that

$$\mathbf{v} = \nabla \times \mathbf{A}.$$

If a vector field v admits a _____ A, then from the equality

$$\nabla \cdot (\nabla \times \mathbf{A}) = 0$$

(divergence of the curl is zero) one obtains

$$\nabla \cdot \mathbf{v} = \nabla \cdot (\nabla \times \mathbf{A}) = 0,$$

which implies that v must be a solenoidal vector field.

a. Lagrangian
b. Vector potential
c. Moment of Inertia
d. Wave equation

14. The _____ specifies the relationship between the two central operations of calculus, differentiation and integration.

The first part of the theorem, sometimes called the first _____, shows that an indefinite integration can be reversed by a differentiation.

The second part, sometimes called the second _____, allows one to compute the definite integral of a function by using any one of its infinitely many antiderivatives.

a. Periodic function
b. Leibniz formula
c. Limits of integration
d. Fundamental Theorem of Calculus

15. In vector calculus, the _____ of a scalar field is a vector field which points in the direction of the greatest rate of increase of the scalar field, and whose magnitude is the greatest rate of change.

A generalization of the _____ for functions on a Euclidean space which have values in another Euclidean space is the Jacobian. A further generalization for a function from one Banach space to another is the Fréchet derivative.

a. Symmetric derivative
b. Lin-Tsien equation
c. Smooth function
d. Gradient

16. Integration is an important concept in mathematics, specifically in the field of calculus and, more broadly, mathematical analysis. Given a function f of a real variable x and an interval [a, b] of the real line, the _____

$$\int_a^b f(x)\,dx,$$

is defined informally to be the net signed area of the region in the xy-plane bounded by the graph of f, the x-axis, and the vertical lines x = a and x = b.

The term '_____' may also refer to the notion of antiderivative, a function F whose derivative is the given function f.

a. Integrand
b. Integral
c. Indefinite integral
d. Integral test for convergence

17. In mathematics, a _____ is an integral where the function to be integrated is evaluated along a curve. Various different line integrals are in use. A specific case of an integration along a closed curve in two dimensions or the complex plane is the contour integral.

Chapter 20. CALCULUS OF VECTOR FIELDS

a. Mittag-Leffler star
c. Line integral
b. Radius of convergence
d. Picard theorem

18. A vector field V defined on a set S is called a _____ or a conservative field if there exists a real valued function (a scalar field) f on S such that

$$V = \nabla f.$$

The associated flow is called the gradient flow, and is used in the method of gradient descent.

The path integral along any closed curve γ (γ(0) = γ(1)) in a _____ is zero:

$$\int_\gamma \langle V(x), dx \rangle = \int_\gamma \langle \nabla f(x), dx \rangle = f(\gamma(1)) - f(\gamma(0))$$

a. Gradient field
c. BIBO stability
b. BDDC
d. 15 theorem

19. In mathematics, the _____ is a representation of a function as an infinite sum of terms calculated from the values of its derivatives at a single point. It may be regarded as the limit of the Taylor polynomials. If the series is centered at zero, the series is also called a Maclaurin series.

a. 15 theorem
c. BIBO stability
b. BDDC
d. Taylor series

20. A quadratic equation with real or complex coefficients has two solutions (or roots), not necessarily distinct, which may or may not be real, given by the _____:

$$\frac{-b \pm \sqrt{b^2 - 4ac}}{2a}$$

Example discriminant signsâ– <0: $x^2+½$â– =0: $-4/_3x^2+4/_3x-1/_3$â– >0: $3/_2x^2+½x-4/_3$

In the above formula, the expression underneath the square root sign

$$D = b^2 - 4ac,$$

is called the discriminant of the quadratic equation.

A quadratic equation with real coefficients can have either one or two distinct real roots, or two distinct complex roots. In this case the discriminant determines the number and nature of the roots.

a. Quadratic formula
c. Quartic function
b. Linear equation
d. Cubic function

21. In geometry, _____ is the division of something into two equal or congruent parts, usually by a line, which is then called a bisector. The most often considered types of bisectors are segment bisectors and angle bisectors. _____ of a line segment using a compass and ruler _____ of an angle using a compass and ruler Line DE bisects line AB at D, line EF is a perpendicular bisector of segment AD at C and the interior bisector of right angle AED

A line segment bisector passes through the midpoint of the segment.

a. BDDC
c. BIBO stability
b. 15 theorem
d. Bisection

22. In mathematics, the _____ is a root-finding algorithm which repeatedly divides an interval in half and then selects the subinterval in which a root exists. It is a very simple and robust method, but it is also rather slow.

Suppose we want to solve the equation

$$f(x) = 0,$$

where f is a continuous function.

a. Bisection method
c. BIBO stability
b. BDDC
d. 15 theorem

23. In mathematics, a function f defined on some set X with real or complex values is a _____ function, if the set of its values is _____. In other words, there exists a number M>0 such that

$$|f(x)| \leq M$$

for all x in X.

Sometimes, if $f(x) \leq A$ for all x in X, then the function is said to be _____ above by A.

a. Bounded
c. Stationary phase approximation
b. Concave upwards
d. Differential coefficient

24. In mathematics, a function f defined on some set X with real or complex values is a _____, if the set of its values is bounded. In other words, there exists a number M>0 such that

$$\boxed{x} >$$

for all x in X.

Sometimes, if ☒ > for all x in X, then the function is said to be bounded above by A.

   a. Bounded Function
   b. Concave downwards
   c. Concave upwards
   d. Power series

25. In mathematics the infimum of a subset of some set is the greatest element, not necessarily in the subset, that is less than or equal to all elements of the subset. Consequently the term _____ is also commonly used. Infima of real numbers are a common special case that is especially important in analysis.
   a. BIBO stability
   b. BDDC
   c. 15 theorem
   d. Greatest lower bound

26. In mathematics, given a subset S of a partially ordered set T, the _____ (sup) of S, if it exists, is the least element of T that is greater than or equal to each element of S. Consequently, the _____ is also referred to as the least upper bound, lub or LUB. If the _____ exists, it may or may not belong to S.
   a. BDDC
   b. Supremum
   c. BIBO stability
   d. 15 theorem

27. In mathematics, especially in order theory, an upper bound of a subset S of some partially ordered set (P, ≤) is an element of P which is greater than or equal to every element of S. The term _____ is defined dually as an element of P which is lesser than or equal to every element of S. A set with an upper bound is said to be bounded from above by that bound, a set with a _____ is said to be bounded from below by that bound.

A subset S of a partially ordered set P may fail to have any bounds or may have many different upper and lower bounds. By transitivity, any element greater than or equal to an upper bound of S is again an upper bound of S, and any element lesser than or equal to any _____ of S is again a _____ of S. This leads to the consideration of least upper bounds: (or suprema) and greatest lower bounds (or infima.)

   a. BDDC
   b. BIBO stability
   c. 15 theorem
   d. Lower bound

28. In mathematics, especially in order theory, an _____ of a subset S of some partially ordered set (P, >≤) is an element of P which is greater than or equal to every element of S. The term lower bound is defined dually as an element of P which is lesser than or equal to every element of S. A set with an _____ is said to be bounded from above by that bound, a set with a lower bound is said to be bounded from below by that bound.

A subset S of a partially ordered set P may fail to have any bounds or may have many different upper and lower bounds. By transitivity, any element greater than or equal to an _____ of S is again an _____ of S, and any element lesser than or equal to any lower bound of S is again a lower bound of S. This leads to the consideration of least upper bounds: (or suprema) and greatest lower bounds (or infima.)

   a. Upper bound
   b. AUSM
   c. ACTRAN
   d. ALGOR

Chapter 20. CALCULUS OF VECTOR FIELDS

29. In mathematics, the _____ is a two-dimensional coordinate system in which each point on a plane is determined by an angle and a distance. The _____ is especially useful in situations where the relationship between two points is most easily expressed in terms of angles and distance; in the more familiar Cartesian or rectangular coordinate system, such a relationship can only be found through trigonometric formulation.

As the coordinate system is two-dimensional, each point is determined by two polar coordinates: the radial coordinate and the angular coordinate.

a. BIBO stability
b. 15 theorem
c. BDDC
d. Polar coordinate system

30. In mathematics, an _____ (or purely _____) is a complex number whose squared value is a real number not greater than zero. The imaginary unit, denoted by i or j, is an example of an _____. If y is a real number, then i · y is an _____, because:

$$(i \cdot y)^2 = i^2 \cdot y^2 = -y^2 \leq 0.$$

Imaginary numbers were defined in 1572 by Rafael Bombelli.

a. Entire function
b. Edge-of-the-wedge theorem
c. Univalent function
d. Imaginary number

31. In mathematics, the complex numbers are an extension of the real numbers obtained by adjoining an imaginary unit, denoted i.

Every _____ can be written in the form a + bi, where a and b are real numbers called the real part and the imaginary part of the _____, respectively.

Complex numbers are a field, and thus have addition, subtraction, multiplication, and division operations. These operations extend the corresponding operations on real numbers, although with a number of additional elegant and useful properties, e.g., negative real numbers can be obtained by squaring complex (imaginary) numbers.

a. Real part
b. Complex number
c. Conjugated line
d. Filled Julia set

32. In mathematics, the _____ of a complex number z, is the second element of the ordered pair of real numbers representing z, i.e. if z = (x,y), or equivalently, z = x + iy, then the _____ of z is y. It is denoted by Im(z) or $\Im\{z\}$, where $\Im$ is a capital I in the Fraktur typeface. The complex function which maps z to the _____ of z is not holomorphic.

a. ACTRAN
b. ALGOR
c. Imaginary unit
d. Imaginary part

Chapter 20. CALCULUS OF VECTOR FIELDS

33. In mathematics, the _____ of a complex number z, is the first element of the ordered pair of real numbers representing z, i.e. if z = (x,y), or equivalently, z = x + iy, then the _____ of z is x. It is denoted by Re{z} or $\Re\{z\}$, where $\Re$ is a capital R in the Fraktur typeface. The complex function which maps z to the _____ of z is not holomorphic.

a. Real part
b. Conjugated line
c. Complex number
d. Filled Julia set

34. In mathematics, the _____ is a geometric representation of the complex numbers established by the real axis and the orthogonal imaginary axis. It can be thought of as a modified Cartesian plane, with the real part of a complex number represented by a displacement along the x-axis, and the imaginary part by a displacement along the y-axis.

The _____ is sometimes called the Argand plane because it is used in Argand diagrams.

a. 15 theorem
b. BDDC
c. BIBO stability
d. Complex plane

Chapter 1
1. d	2. d	3. d	4. d	5. d	6. c	7. d	8. d	9. d	10. d
11. d	12. d	13. d	14. d	15. b	16. a	17. d	18. d	19. d	20. c
21. a	22. a	23. c	24. b	25. b	26. a	27. b	28. b	29. d	30. b
31. b	32. d	33. b	34. d	35. d	36. d	37. d	38. d	39. d	40. d
41. d	42. b	43. d	44. a	45. b	46. d	47. c	48. c	49. d	50. d
51. b	52. d	53. d	54. b						

Chapter 2
1. c	2. d	3. b	4. d	5. b	6. d	7. d	8. d	9. d	10. b
11. a	12. a	13. a	14. b	15. b	16. b	17. c	18. c	19. d	20. b
21. c	22. a								

Chapter 3
1. c	2. d	3. d	4. d	5. d	6. d	7. d	8. d	9. a	10. a
11. d	12. d	13. d	14. d	15. d	16. d	17. a	18. c	19. d	20. d
21. b	22. d	23. d	24. a	25. d	26. b	27. c	28. d	29. a	30. a
31. b	32. d	33. a							

Chapter 4
1. d	2. a	3. d	4. b	5. a	6. d	7. d	8. d	9. d	10. a
11. d	12. d	13. d	14. c	15. d	16. d	17. a	18. c	19. a	20. d
21. d	22. d	23. d	24. a	25. c	26. a	27. d	28. b	29. d	30. d
31. d									

Chapter 5
1. d	2. d	3. c	4. b	5. b	6. d	7. c	8. c	9. b	10. d
11. b	12. d	13. a							

Chapter 6
1. b	2. c	3. d	4. d	5. d	6. d	7. c	8. c	9. d	10. d
11. c	12. c	13. d							

Chapter 7
1. a	2. a	3. d	4. d	5. d	6. b	7. d	8. c	9. b	10. d
11. a	12. d	13. b	14. d	15. b	16. d	17. c	18. a	19. a	20. d
21. c	22. d	23. a	24. d	25. d	26. c	27. d	28. c	29. d	30. b
31. d	32. d	33. d							

Chapter 8
1. d	2. a	3. b	4. a	5. d	6. a	7. c	8. d	9. b	10. a
11. b	12. b	13. d	14. c	15. c	16. c	17. d	18. b	19. a	20. d
21. d	22. b	23. a							

ANSWER KEY

Chapter 9
1. d   2. d   3. d   4. c   5. d   6. d   7. d   8. c   9. d   10. b
11. b   12. a   13. d   14. d   15. d   16. d   17. a   18. c

Chapter 10
1. d   2. a   3. d   4. a   5. d   6. d   7. c   8. a   9. d   10. c
11. a   12. c   13. d   14. d   15. d   16. a   17. b   18. b   19. d   20. c
21. a   22. c   23. d   24. c

Chapter 11
1. a   2. d   3. b   4. c   5. d   6. c   7. b   8. a   9. d   10. a
11. a   12. d   13. d   14. c   15. c   16. a   17. d   18. c   19. d   20. c
21. d   22. d   23. b   24. b   25. d   26. d   27. d   28. d   29. c   30. d
31. d   32. d   33. b   34. b

Chapter 12
1. d   2. c   3. b   4. b   5. d   6. d   7. d   8. a   9. d   10. c
11. c   12. a   13. d   14. c   15. c   16. c   17. c   18. d   19. d   20. c

Chapter 13
1. d   2. b   3. d   4. b   5. a   6. d   7. d   8. b   9. d   10. b
11. b   12. b   13. a   14. c   15. a   16. d   17. d   18. d   19. b   20. d

Chapter 14
1. b   2. d   3. d   4. b   5. a   6. d   7. d   8. b   9. b   10. c
11. c   12. d   13. d   14. b   15. d   16. a   17. d   18. c   19. d   20. d
21. d   22. d   23. d   24. c

Chapter 15
1. d   2. d   3. d   4. a   5. b   6. d   7. d   8. c   9. d   10. c
11. d   12. c   13. d   14. b   15. b   16. d   17. d   18. c   19. a   20. d
21. d

Chapter 16
1. b   2. d   3. d   4. d   5. d   6. d   7. d   8. a   9. a   10. b
11. d   12. d   13. b   14. d   15. d   16. b

Chapter 17
1. d   2. d   3. d   4. d   5. d   6. a   7. a   8. d   9. a   10. b
11. d   12. d   13. d   14. d   15. c   16. d   17. c   18. d   19. b   20. b
21. d

Chapter 18
1. d   2. a   3. d   4. b   5. b   6. d   7. d   8. b   9. d   10. d
11. a   12. d   13. b   14. d   15. a   16. b   17. c

Chapter 19
1. d   2. b   3. c   4. b   5. d   6. d   7. d   8. a   9. d   10. d

Chapter 20
1. c   2. d   3. d   4. d   5. d   6. a   7. c   8. d   9. c   10. a
11. b   12. d   13. b   14. d   15. d   16. b   17. c   18. a   19. d   20. a
21. d   22. a   23. a   24. a   25. d   26. b   27. d   28. a   29. d   30. d
31. b   32. d   33. a   34. d

www.ingramcontent.com/pod-product-compliance
Lightning Source LLC
Chambersburg PA
CBHW082043230426
43670CB00016B/2759